MAINE TRIVIA

MAINE TRIVIA

JOHN N. COLE

Rutledge Hill Press®
Nashville, Tennessee

Published in Nashville, Tennessee, by Rutledge Hill Press®,
211 Seventh Avenue North, Nashville, Tennessee 37219.
Distributed in Canada by H. B. Fenn & Company, Ltd.,
34 Nixon Road, Bolton, Ontario L7E 1W2.
Distributed in Australia by The Five Mile Press Pty., Ltd.,
22 Summit Road, Noble Park, Victoria 3174.
Distributed in New Zealand by Tandem Press, 2 Rugby Road,
Birkenhead, Auckland 10.
Distributed in the United Kingdom by Verulam Publishing, Ltd.,
152a Park Street Lane, Park Street,
St. Albans, Hertfordshire AL2 2AU.

Typography by Compass Communications, Inc., Nashville, Tennessee.

Library of Congress Cataloging-in-Publication Data
Cole, John N., 1923–
    Maine trivia / John N. Cole.
        p.   cm.
    ISBN 1-55853-603-5 (pb)
    1. Maine—Miscellanea.   II. Title.
F19.C73   1998
977.1—dc21   98-2977
                                                                CIP

Printed in the United States of America.
1 2 3 4 5 6 7 8 9 — 02 01 00 99 98

PREFACE

Maine people have always had a strong sense of place. Perhaps this began with geography, for its being located as it is in the farthest northeast corner of the United States. Maine started out as a place apart, a state where independence has flourished for almost two hundred years. Living with twenty million acres of forest and more than three thousand miles of rugged North Atlantic coast has endowed Maine people with a rare and refreshing integrity. And it is this unabashed honesty, this direct way of looking at life and dealing with people that is the state's greatest treasure. If you begin with this premise as you turn this book's pages, you can learn a good deal worth knowing about this very special place.

TABLE OF CONTENTS

ACKNOWLEDGMENTS

No one person ever wrote a book. It's always a job that requires help, this book more so than many. It could never have been written without the constant work and encouragement of my wife, Jean, who spent countless hours acquiring and relaying much of the information in these pages.

And then there are Brian and Laura of Brunswick's Curtis Memorial Library. Without their knowledge of where and how to look and their selfless gift of time on my behalf, I'd still be lost in the stacks.

My grateful and everlasting thanks to these angels and to each of the others who sat on my shoulder. I'm a lucky man.

MAINE TRIVIA

GEOGRAPHY

C H A P T E R O N E

Q. What percentage of Maine's total area is water?

A. 10 percent.

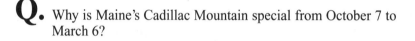

Q. Why is Maine's Cadillac Mountain special from October 7 to March 6?

A. It's the first land in the United States touched by the rays of the rising sun.

Q. Where is the world's largest boulder?

A. Fryeburg.

Q. Where are the Calendar Islands?

A. Casco Bay.

Q. Which Maine island was once known as "the Coney Island of the East"?

A. Peaks, in Casco Bay.

Q. Which Maine town has the longest growing season?

A. Eastport, where the average time between frosts is 175 days.

Q. Which town has the shortest growing season?

A. Squa Pan, where you can rely on just seventy-five days.

Q. What five rivers meet in Merrymeeting Bay?

A. Kennebec, Androscoggin, Cathance, Abbacadasset, and Eastern.

Q. What is the source of the Androscoggin River?

A. Lake Umbagog.

Q. What percentage of Maine is forested?

A. 80 percent.

Q. What is Maine's easternmost community?

A. Lubec.

Q. How many miles of rivers and streams flow through Maine?

A. About thirty-two thousand.

Q. Maine contains how many lakes and ponds?

A. Six thousand.

———⸺———

Q. What is the most frequently used name for ponds in the state?

A. Mud Pond.

———⸺———

Q. On a clear day where in Maine can you get the best view of New Hampshire's Mount Washington?

A. Atop Mount Agamenticus, in York.

———⸺———

Q. What is the only state that borders Maine?

A. New Hampshire.

———⸺———

Q. How long is the border shared by Maine and Canada?

A. 611 miles.

———⸺———

Q. How many U.S. Customs stations are there along the U.S.-Canadian border?

A. Twenty-nine: twenty-six on the land and three at seaports and airports.

———⸺———

Q. What is the largest lake lying wholly within the state?

A. Moosehead (117 square miles).

Q. What is Maine's largest city?

A. Portland (population 64,358, according to 1990 census).

———

Q. Where does Portland get its drinking water?

A. Sebago Lake.

———

Q. Where in Maine is the largest single land area devoted solely to wilderness uses?

A. Baxter Sate Park, whose entire 201,018 acres—including Mount Katahdin—were given to the state by Gov. Percival P. Baxter in the 1930s.

———

Q. What is Maine's highest mountain?

A. Katahdin, at 5,267 feet above sea level.

———

Q. How long is the Maine coast?

A. Measured as the crow flies, it's about 225 miles; but it's more than 3,500 miles by foot.

———

Q. What is the largest county in Maine?

A. Aroostook, in northeastern Maine (6,821 square miles).

———

Q. What is Maine's second-largest lake?

A. Sebago (44.8 square miles).

Q. What Maine town is halfway between the North Pole and the equator?

A. Perry.

———⊗∞⊗———

Q. Which Maine bog has been designated a national landmark?

A. Orono Bog.

———⊗∞⊗———

Q. What is Maine's least-populated county?

A. Piscataquis, with four people per square mile.

———⊗∞⊗———

Q. Public beaches comprise how many miles of Maine's coastline?

A. Seventy-four.

———⊗∞⊗———

Q. Off the coast of Maine are how many islands?

A. Approximately thirty-five hundred.

———⊗∞⊗———

Q. Primarily responsible for the varied Maine topography was what geological event?

A. The great gouging glaciers of the Ice Age.

———⊗∞⊗———

Q. What are Maine's five largest islands?

A. Mount Desert (ponounced de-SERT), Deer Isle, Vinalhaven, Georgetown, and Isleboro.

Q. How many of Maine's mountains are more than thirty-four hundred feet high?

A. Fifty.

———⊗∞⊗———

Q. What Maine coastal community has the state's highest tides?

A. Eastport, where mean high tides rise 18.2 feet.

———⊗∞⊗———

Q. Maine has how many counties?

A. Sixteen.

———⊗∞⊗———

Q. How much of Maine is defined as "unorganized territory"?

A. 44 percent (with an approximate population of fewer than ten thousand people).

———⊗∞⊗———

Q. Who was the first person to map what is now the Maine coast?

A. Capt. John Smith, in 1614.

———⊗∞⊗———

Q. How much of Maine's landmass is underwater?

A. 1.58 million acres, covered by lakes, ponds, rivers, brooks, and inland waterways.

———⊗∞⊗———

Q. What are the southernmost Maine islands?

A. Appledore, Smulty Nose, Malaga, Cedar, and Duck (also known as the Isles of Shoals off Portsmouth, New Hampshire).

Q. The Isles of Shoals originally had what name?

A. Smith's Isles.

Q. What is Maine's most-populated county?

A. Cumberland.

Q. Appledore Island was first called by what name?

A. Hog Island, one of the most popular names for islands along the Maine coast.

Q. What three Maine counties honor heroes of the American Revolution?

A. Knox, Hancock, and Washington.

Q. What is the only community in Maine that has the same name as a city in Spain?

A. Madrid, pronounced MAD-rid, not ma-DRID.

Q. Why do the Calendar Islands have that name?

A. There are 365 of them.

Q. What Maine coastal community is named after a French port?

A. Calais, pronounced KAL-is.

Q. Of the more than four hundred municipalities in Maine, how many are designated as cities?

A. Twenty-two: Auburn, Augusta (the capital), Bangor, Bath, Belfast, Biddeford, Brewer, Calais, Caribou, Eastport, Ellsworth, Gardiner, Hallowell, Lewiston, Old Town, Portland, Presque Isle, Rockland, Saco, South Portland, Waterville, and Westbrook.

Q. How much of Maine is peat bog?

A. An estimated seven hundred thousand acres.

Q. How does a Maine community become a city?

A. It initiates a request to the state legislature, which can then pass an act of incorporation. There are no special requirements.

Q. What percentage of Maine's residents live in its cities?

A. About 30 percent.

Q. What is the correct way to pronounce Saco?

A. SOCK-oh.

Q. What is special about Babb's Bridge?

A. It's Maine oldest covered bridge, built across the Presumpscot River in 1840 to connect Gorham and Windham.

Q. Maine ranks in what order among the fifty states in land area?

A. Thirty-ninth.

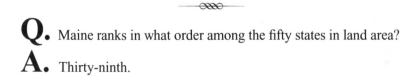

Q. How long is the Allagash Wilderness Waterway?

A. Ninety-two miles, flowing through Aroostook and Piscataquis Counties.

Q. Captain Kidd's treasure is reported to be buried on what Casco Bay island?

A. Jewell, the most worked-over site in Maine by treasure hunters.

Q. Where did the pirate captain Samuel Bellamy plan to found a "pirate republic" in Maine?

A. Machias (ma-CHY-as), but he was hanged before he could do so.

Q. Richardson, Mooselookmeguntick, and Cupsuptic are part of what chain of lakes?

A. Rangeley Lakes, first visited by explorers in 1794.

Q. To find Pamola Peak, Knife Edge, and the Tableland, where would you go?

A. Mount Katahdin in Baxter State Park. The three are distinct physical features of the mountain.

Q. Where is Lily Bay State Park?

A. On the eastern shore of Moosehead Lake, about ten miles north of Greenville.

Q. What is the smallest Maine county?

A. Sagadahoc, at just 257 square miles.

Q. When people say, "At Perry it's deep red, at Bailey's Mistake it's black, at Jonesport it's brilliant white," what are they talking about?

A. Sand. These Washington County communities have beaches with distinctly different-colored sand.

Q. What are the Native-American names for three lakes in the Rangeley chain?

A. Welokennebacook, Aldabendabagog, and Molechunkamunk.

Q. What river flows between Bucksport and Bangor?

A. Penobscot.

Q. What was the state's first county?

A. York, created in 1652 and officially incorporated as York County in 1760.

Q. The title "the Worm Center of the World" belongs to what Maine village?

A. Wiscasset.

Q. What is known as "the Grand Canyon of Maine"?

A. Gulf Hagas.

Q. How far is it from Eastport to Lubec by boat?

A. Three miles, but forty by car.

Q. Quoddy Head State Park contains how many acres?

A. Four hundred.

———∞∞∞———

Q. The nation's first forest-fire lookout tower was built on what mountain?

A. Squaw, in 1905.

———∞∞∞———

Q. What is Maine's longest county?

A. Somerset, extending 150 miles from the Canadian border to Fairfield.

———∞∞∞———

Q. What town is known as "the Home of Famous Sea Captains"?

A. Searsport, Maine's second-busiest seaport and home of the Penobscot Marine Museum.

———∞∞∞———

Q. What is Maine's busiest seaport?

A. Portland.

———∞∞∞———

Q. When Downeasters speak about "Old Sow," what are they talking about?

A. One of the world's largest whirlpools, in Passamaquoddy Bay.

———∞∞∞———

Q. Where is North America's only fjord?

A. Mount Desert Island.

Q. When was the first limestone quarry opened in Maine?

A. 1733 in Thomaston, now the home of the Maine State Prison.

Q. What is the smallest town in Maine?

A. Bowerbank, population twenty-seven (as of 1998).

Q. What is the second-busiest oil port on the East Coast?

A. Portland.

Q. What is special about Peter Dana Point?

A. It's a Native-American reservation.

Q. What is the name of Maine's largest hydroelectric dam?

A. Wyman, completed in 1931.

Q. How many Maine counties have Native-American names?

A. Six: Androscoggin, Aroostook, Kennebec, Penobscot, Piscataquis, and Sagadahoc.

Q. Where is a desert to be found in Maine?

A. Freeport, where a once-fertile farm disappeared under glacial sand that had been covered by a thin layer of topsoil.

Q. Capt. John Smith used what Maine island as a fishing base?

A. Monhegan, one of the outermost islands on the coast.

Q. What is the English translation of *Katahdin,* a Native-American name?

A. "Greatest mountain."

Q. Where in Maine is North Bubble Mountain?

A. Acadia National Park.

Q. What was the first capital of the state?

A. Portland.

Q. What is the present capital?

A. Augusta, where it was moved from Portland in 1832.

Q. How many years ago did the great glaciers retreat from the Maine coast?

A. Twelve thousand.

Q. The source of the Kennebec River is what lake?

A. Moosehead.

Q. Where is the nation's only cribstone bridge?

A. Connecting Orr's and Bailey Islands in Casco Bay, built entirely of granite blocks without mortar.

Q. What are glacial cirques?

A. Deep three-sided ravines formed by vast accumulations of snow during the Ice Age. They are among Mount Katahdin's most distinctive features.

Q. What is the official state fossil?

A. *Pertica quadrifaria.*

Q. The first townships established in Maine had what dimensions?

A. Six miles square (many still are).

Q. Where were the nation's first logging camps?

A. Penobscot River, in the 1830s.

Q. How large were the trees when logging began?

A. Up to two hundred feet tall and ten feet in diameter.

Q. Where was the nation's first gold strike?

A. Swift River in Byron, where panners still search for gold.

Q. Where is "the Moxie Capital of the World"?

A. Frank Anicetti's Kennebec Fruit Company in Lisbon Falls.

Q. Which Maine community did White Russian expatriates believe has a climate much like Moscow's?

A. Richmond, on the banks of the lower Kennebec. It was settled by Russians in the 1940s.

Q. What is Maine's largest state-owned island?

A. Swan, the game sanctuary in Merrymeeting Bay.

Q. Who gave Isle au Haut its name?

A. French navigator Samuel de Champlain, in 1604. (It means "high island.")

Q. What is most notable about the lighthouse at West Quoddy Head?

A. It stands at the easternmost point in the United Sates.

Q. Why are the Reversing Falls so named?

A. The falls, where Denny and Whiting Bays squeeze into Cobsook Bay, flow one way and then the other with every shift of the region's extreme tides.

Q. What is the correct pronunciation of Piscataquis?

A. Pis-CAT-a-kwiss.

Q. Where is the Lumberman's Museum?

A. Just west of Patten.

———∽∞∾———

Q. Why did Maine's Native Americans travel from afar to Mount Kineo?

A. To gather the mountain's fine flint for arrowheads, tools, and weapons.

———∽∞∾———

Q. Which Maine county is larger than Rhode Island and Connecticut combined?

A. Aroostook.

———∽∞∾———

Q. What is Marginal Way?

A. A mile-long footpath on a cliff that overlooks the sea at Ogunquit, donated to the town in 1923 by the farmer who owned the land.

———∽∞∾———

Q. Where is the four-thousand-acre Rachel Carson National Wildlife Refuge?

A. Wells, just north of the Laudholm Farm.

———∽∞∾———

Q. What kind of park is Ocean Park?

A. Educational summer resort founded by Free Will Baptists. Ocean Park is near Old Orchard Beach.

———∽∞∾———

Q. What are the Songo Locks?

A. A network of twenty-seven locks in the canal that links Sebago Lake to Brandy Pond and Long Lake.

Q. Scattered throughout the state, what are "horsebacks"?

A. Conspicuous ridges of sand and gravel left by glaciers.

Q. What excursion boat plies the Songo Locks?

A. *Songo River Queen.*

Q. What Washington County crop makes a good pie?

A. Blueberries. (Maine grows more than any other state.)

Q. What is the highest point of coastal land between Canada and Brazil?

A. Cadillac Mountain, in Acadia National Park (1,530 feet).

Q. What was known in the nineteenth century as the Maine Turnpike?

A. The ocean route from the Maine coast to Boston, called such by merchants and sailors.

Q. What are Maine's four geographical regions?

A. Coastal Maine, Corridor Maine, the Aroostook Region, and the Interior Region.

Q. Maine potatoes come from what county?

A. Aroostook.

Q. What is a drumlin?

A. A hill shaped like an upside-down spoon, formed of especially sticky clay by the glaciers, which smeared them across much of coastal Maine.

Q. The most snow falls in what month?

A. January, an average of nineteen inches of snow over the past thirty years.

Q. What's the state's record cold temperature?

A. Forty-eight degrees below zero in Van Buren, on January 19, 1925.

Q. What portion of Maine land is publicly owned?

A. 2 percent, the smallest percentage of any state in the nation.

Q. What is Maine's most popular public recreation area?

A. Acadia National Park on Mount Desert Island, which accounts for 60 percent of all visitor days in all public areas.

Q. What is Maine's busiest airport?

A. Portland International.

Q. What is a tarn?

A. A lake at the bottom of a glacial cirque (such as Chimney Pond at Mount Katahdin).

Q. In which direction do most of the grooves and scratches in Maine rocks trend?

A. Southeast, because that's the direction the glaciers were moving when they slid toward the sea.

Q. When you climb South Bubble in Acadia, what do you find?

A. Balanced Rock, a large boulder called an erratic, perched on a peak.

Q. How much gold is stored at Maine's Fort Knox?

A. None. Begun in 1844, the granite fort still overlooks the Penobscot River across from Bucksport. It is named after Revolutionary War Gen. Henry Knox.

Q. How high is the gravel ridge known as the Enfield Horseback?

A. Fifty feet. The road along its crest is six miles long.

Q. What Maine city was first named Machigonne?

A. Portland.

Q. Where is the summer home of the forty-first president of the United States?

A. Walker's Point, Kennebunkport, where George and Barbara Bush vacation.

Q. What is the Carson Trail?

A. A mile-long nature trail open to the public at the Rachel Carson National Wildlife Refuge.

Q. Where does Maine rank in size (area) among the New England states?

A. First.

Q. What province is Maine's close Canadian neighbor?

A. Quebec.

Q. The expression "Down East" to describe Maine comes from what source?

A. Early New Englanders used the word *down* to mean north, so sailors voyaging to Maine from Boston said they were sailing "down east."

Q. What mountains stretch across much of northwest Maine?

A. White.

Q. What is Maine's major transportation artery?

A. Interstate Highway 95, which runs 303 miles from Kittery to Houlton.

Q. What is Maine's principal dry cargo port?

A. Searsport.

Q. How many miles of railroad tracks still operate in Maine?

A. Twelve hundred.

Q. What is the *Bluenose*?

A. A ferry that sails year-round from Bar Harbor to Yarmouth, Nova Scotia.

Q. Where is Spencer Bay?

A. On the eastern shore of Moosehead Lake, as is Uly Bay and Beaver Cove.

Q. What river separates Lewiston from Auburn and Topsham from Brunswick?

A. Androscoggin.

Q. The granite used to build the towers of New York City's Triboro Bridge came from what Maine source?

A. Quarries on Vinalhaven Island.

Q. How many Maine locales are named for animals?

A. 302.

Q. How many ponds named Round are in Maine?

A. Thirty-two.

Q. What Maine island was the source of the granite used to construct the U.S. Treasury Building in Washington, D.C.?

A. Dix.

Q. Where did Maine's largest iron mine operate from 1843 to 1856?

A. At the foot of Mount Katahdin.

Q. How many granite quarries once flourished in Maine?

A. Nearly one hundred. Until the advent of concrete, steel, and glass, granite was the nation's basic building material for foundations, steps, and monuments.

Q. Maine's slate deposits are concentrated in what county?

A. Piscataquis.

Q. What are Maine's six Class A salmon rivers?

A. Dennys, Ducktrap, East Machias, Narraguagus, Pleasant, and Sheepscot.

Q. What organization classifies Maine's rivers?

A. Atlantic Salmon Commission, because these rivers support runs of wild Atlantic salmon.

Q. From what material is the roof of New York's Saint Patrick's Cathedral made?

A. Maine slate.

Q. What is Maine's fourth-largest lake?

A. Flagstaff.

Q. What is Mooselookmeguntic?

A. Maine's fifth-largest lake (25.9 square miles). Of Abenaki origin, the name means "moose feeding among big trees" or "portage to the moose feeding place."

Q. How many Lost Ponds are in Maine?

A. Twenty-one.

Q. Before a dam created the lake that flooded their community, how many people lived in Flagstaff?

A. About three hundred.

Q. How many seaplane bases are in Maine?

A. Seventeen, most of them in Moosehead Lake.

Q. How many Black Brooks are there in Maine?

A. Twenty-three.

Q. What is Maine's longest river?

A. Saint John (331 miles, with its southwest branch).

Q. Where does Maine rank among the states in abundance of semiprecious gemstones?

A. First.

Q. Maine has how many miles of rivers and streams?

A. 5,151.

Q. Where was the world's largest emerald beryl discovered?

A. Bumpers Mine, in Lynchville.

Q. How many Maine rivers are longer than twenty miles?

A. Seventy-three.

Q. What lucky find led prospectors to pan for gold in the Swift River?

A. A farmer found gold dust in the crop of a chicken that had been pecking along the riverbank.

Q. Men removed more than six million tons of what resource from the Kennebec River in 1896?

A. Ice.

Q. How much tidal water moves in and out of Passamaquoddy Bay every twenty-four hours?

A. Eight billion tons.

Q. What was special about Kennebec River ice?

A. It was said to be the purest in the world.

Q. Why is Maine an especially good place from which to view the northern lights (aurora borealis)?

A. It is one of the northernmost states and has so few cities whose lights can often obscure the display.

Q. After whom is Cadillac Mountain named?

A. Sieur Antoine de la Mothe Cadillac, the early-eighteenth-century proprietor of Mount Desert Island.

Q. Who gave Mount Desert its name?

A. French explorer Samuel de Champlain, who called it L'Isle des Monts Deserts (island of barren mountains) because there was no vegetation on its mountaintops.

Q. How old are the Mount Desert mountains that rise from the sea?

A. About four hundred million years.

Q. Mount Desert Island contains how many mountains?

A. Seventeen.

Q. Where is Maine's largest saltwater marsh?

A. Scarborough.

Q. To settle a lawsuit in 1977, what Native-American tribes were awarded 12.5 million acres of Maine land?

A. Penobscot, Passamaquoddy, and Maleseet.

Q. Where did the first transatlantic balloon flight begin?

A. Presque Isle, in 1978.

Q. What town was ravaged by a great fire in October 1947?

A. Bar Harbor.

Q. What Maine town is known as "the Sardine Capital of the World"?

A. Eastport.

Q. Penobscot County was formed in what year?

A. 1816.

Q. Who first explored the Maine coast?

A. Leif Eriksson, in 1003.

Q. How many Trout Ponds and Beaver Ponds are found in Maine?

A. Fourteen named Trout Pond and twenty-four named Beaver Pond.

Q. What was Bar Harbor's original name?

A. Eden.

Q. Maine has how many public fishing piers?

A. Eight.

Q. What is the earliest date the ice has made its annual exit from Moosehead Lake?

A. April 14, in 1954.

Q. At what town is one of the world's few beaches composed entirely of jasper pebbles?

A. Machiasport, home of Jasper Beach.

Q. What and where is the Great Heath?

A. A peat bog in Washington County.

Q. Over how much of Maine are black bears found?

A. About 80 percent.

Q. How many square miles does Maine encompass?

A. 33,265.

Q. Thirty miles off the Maine coast, what two ocean currents meet?

A. Arctic Current and Gulf Stream.

Q. Matinicus Island is part of an archipelago containing what five other islands?

A. Criehaven, Wooden Ball, Seal, No Man's, and Twobush.

Q. How many acres does Matinicus Island comprise?

A. 720.

Q. Aroostook County contains how many square miles?

A. 6,453.

Q. What is the latest date the ice has made its annual exit from Moosehead Lake?

A. May 29, in 1878.

Q. The state's only bridge that is completely covered by shingles is in what community?

A. Robyville Village, crossing Kenduskeag stream, built in 1876.

Q. Where is the largest Denil fishway in the nation?

A. Saint Croix River, at Woodland.

Q. Where are Maine's most productive oyster beds?

A. The bottom of Salt Bay in the Damariscotta River.

Q. How long is Big Deer Isle?

A. Nine miles.

Q. The northern terminus of the Appalachian Trail is on what mountain?

A. Katahdin.

Q. What is the highest village in Maine?

A. Paris Hill, 831 feet above sea level.

Q. Why did Christmas Cove receive that name?

A. John Smith anchored his ship there on Christmas Day 1614.

Q. How do you pronounce the Maine town named Seboeis?

A. SEE-boys.

Q. Feldspar is most plentiful in what region of Maine?

A. Paris-Newry.

Q. The only canal ever built in Maine runs between what two locations?

A. Sebago Lake and Portland, the Cumberland and Oxford Canal.

Q. What was the earliest French possession in North America?

A. Dochet's Island in the Saint Croix River, claimed in 1604.

Q. What is the most photographed house in Maine?

A. Wedding Cake House, in Kennebunk.

ENTERTAINMENT

C H A P T E R   T W O

Q. Who was Holman Day?

A. One of Maine's most prolific filmmakers, who made thirty-five two-reel silent movies in the 1920s.

Q. What Maine singer entertained troops during World War II?

A. Reta Shaw of South Paris, who also played guitar.

Q. Crooner Rudy Vallee grew up in what Maine community?

A. Westbrook, where his father had a drugstore and soda fountain.

Q. In what year did actress Sarah Bernhardt visit Portland?

A. 1906.

Q. Who played Gov. Percival Baxter in one of Holman Day's movies?

A. Percival Baxter, governor of Maine.

Q. Where is the Temple Theater?

A. Houlton, where it has shown movies since it was built in 1919.

Q. Who owned the first commercial radio station in Maine?

A. Henry P. Rines, the original owner-operator of WCSH-AM in Portland, licensed in June 1925.

Q. What Maine theater was proclaimed the official state theater by the legislature?

A. Lakewood Theater in Madison, in 1967.

Q. The Stonington High School championship basketball team played at what venue in the 1930s?

A. Stonington Opera House.

Q. What movie palace was the only one in New England in 1929 to have its own power system?

A. State Theater in Portland.

Q. When was the first Cumberland County Fair held?

A. October 10–11, 1868.

Q. What Native-American chief appeared in more than fifty silent films?

A. Algonquin chieftain Henry "Red Eagle" Parly, of Greenville.

Q. What is Bobo the Clown's real name?

A. Ron Starkey (he lives in Biddeford and has been a clown in Greater Portland since 1980).

Q. How much beer do Maine residents consume each year?

A. About twenty-six million gallons.

Q. Why is Allen's Coffee Brandy the best-selling hard liquor in Maine?

A. Lobstermen use it to preserve their bait.

Q. What was the first curb service drive-in to open in Caribou?

A. Sesme Car Hop, opened July 4, 1956.

Q. In 1920 D. W. Griffith made what movie about Maine?

A. *Way Down East,* photographed in Connecticut.

Q. In the *Bert and I* recordings of Maine stories, who supplied the voice of "I"?

A. Marshall Dodge.

Q. Tony Curtis portrayed what real-life person in the film *The Great Impostor*?

A. Impersonator Ferdinand N. Demarra Jr., whose last impersonation was as a teacher at the North Haven grade school.

Q. What was "the Drama Law of 1750"?

A. A Maine and Massachusetts law prohibiting theatrical performances because "they have a pernicious influence on the minds of young people."

———— ∞∞ ————

Q. What is a Bean-Hole Supper?

A. A popular evening event and fundraiser among Maine church groups and social service organizations.

———— ∞∞ ————

Q. What was the cost of admission to the Cumberland Fair in 1872?

A. One dime.

———— ∞∞ ————

Q. Where did TV star Linda Lavin *(Alice)* go to school?

A. Wayneflete, a private school in Portland.

———— ∞∞ ————

Q. What do the call letters of WCBB, Maine's public television station, stand for?

A. Colby, Bates, and Bowdoin—Maine's three private colleges that sponsor the station.

———— ∞∞ ————

Q. Who was the hostess of TV's *Romper Room* during the 1970s?

A. Connie Roussin Spann, of Lewiston.

———— ∞∞ ————

Q. What was a husking bee?

A. A social event in colonial rural Maine in which neighbors gathered to husk the corn after it was harvested and the ears piled around the barn.

Q. What do the call letters of WCSH-TV, the NBC affiliate in Portland, stand for?

A. Congress Square Hotel, owned by the founder of WCSH radio and television.

Q. As of 1998, who was Maine's longest-working television news anchor?

A. Kim Block, of Portland's WGME-TV, anchoring since December 20, 1980.

Q. Where did Maine's first radio broadcast originate?

A. A Bangor church, in 1922.

Q. When was the first motion picture shown in Maine?

A. 1910.

Q. What was the title of the movie version of Maine author Ruth Moore's novel *Spoonhandle*?

A. *Deep Waters.*

Q. What Maine summer theater calls itself "America's Foremost Summer Theater"?

A. Ogunquit Playhouse.

Q. What happened when a guy found a red ear of corn at a colonial husking bee?

A. He had the right to kiss each girl at the gathering.

Q. What traveling show toured Maine's remote Franklin County in the early 1900s?

A. Al Martz Minstrels.

Q. What stage event was performed to celebrate the 1928 dedication of the new Cariton Bridge across the Kennebec River at Bath?

A. *A Pageant of the State of Maine,* a two-hour show.

Q. Who starred in *Deep Water,* filmed in Vinalhaven?

A. Jose Ferrer and Dana Andrews.

Q. Who won an Academy Award in 1940 for directing *The Grapes of Wrath?*

A. John Ford, of Portland.

Q. Where was the movie version of *Carousel* filmed in 1955, starring Gordon MacRae?

A. Boothbay Harbor.

Q. What were the box office receipts for the movie *Showboat* when it was shown on July 11, 1936, at the Lakeside Theater in Rangeley?

A. $197.20 for both the matinee and evening shows.

Q. What was Witch Way?

A. The Cape Elizabeth home of Bette Davis and her husband, Gary Merrill, during the 1950s.

Q. Where was the movie *On Golden Pond* originally planned to be filmed?

A. Great Pond, in Belgrade.

———∞∞∞———

Q. What play, starring Bette Davis and Gary Merrill, had its world premiere at Portland's State Theater in September 1959?

A. *The World of Carl Sandburg.*

———∞∞∞———

Q. On January 3, 1943, what radio star broadcast his show live from Maine?

A. Jack Benny, at Dow Air Force Base in Bangor.

———∞∞∞———

Q. Which Maine actress starred in *The Longest Night*?

A. Phyllis Thaxter, of Cumberland Foreside.

———∞∞∞———

Q. What Broadway musical starred Downeaster Rudy Vallee?

A. *How to Succeed in Business Without Really Trying,* in 1961.

———∞∞∞———

Q. What is served at a Maine dinner party when a guest requests a scrid?

A. A small portion.

———∞∞∞———

Q. Where is the world's largest frying pan?

A. Pittsfield, where the 10.5-foot-diameter pan is used annually the last Saturday in July during the Central Maine Egg Festival.

Q. What Portland-born woman was known as "Axis Sally," a Nazi propaganda broadcaster during World War II?

A. Mildred Elizabeth Gillars, born on November 29, 1900.

Q. What does the Old Port Festival celebrate every June?

A. Portland's revitalization, with a huge block party.

Q. Who popularized "Stein Song," the official University of Maine song?

A. Rudy Vallee.

Q. Where is the Maine State Music Theater?

A. Bowdoin College, in Brunswick.

Q. What event commemorates Maine's two-foot-gauge railroad history?

A. Maine Narrow Gauge Railroad Days, in Boothbay in September.

Q. For whom is the Portland City Hall Auditorium's organ named?

A. Herman Kotzschmar, a nineteenth-century organist/composer and friend of publishing magnate Cyrus Curtis, who in 1912 donated the funds for the sixty-thousand-dollar organ.

Q. When Portland became the first city in America to hire a municipal organist, who was chosen?

A. Composer William C. MacFarlane, composer of "America the Beautiful."

Q. Where in Maine was Elvis scheduled to appear just two days after he died?

A. Augusta Civic Center.

———— ✺ ————

Q. What was the sign illuminated on the movie screen before every showing at the Lakeside Theater in Rangeley during the 1930s?

A. "Ladies, Please Remove Your Hats. Gentlemen, Please Don't Spit on the Floor."

———— ✺ ————

Q. What band played at the Claremont Hotel's one hundredth anniversary celebration in 1984?

A. The Royal River Philharmonic Jazz Band, from Yarmouth.

———— ✺ ————

Q. What store served Moxie Ice Cream cones?

A. Kennebec Fruit Company, in Lisbon Falls.

———— ✺ ————

Q. When is Moxie Day in Lisbon Falls?

A. Second Saturday in July.

———— ✺ ————

Q. Who first introduced fudge to Rumford?

A. Charles Eli Howe, at his store in 1900.

———— ✺ ————

Q. How many stools were available at the counter of Jack's Lunch, in Bath, in 1923?

A. Ten.

Q. Which member of the trio Peter, Paul, and Mary lives in Blue Hill?

A. Paul Stookey.

———∞∞∞———

Q. What was the best-selling confection at the Houlton Dairy Bar during the summer of 1994?

A. Brownie à la Mode.

———∞∞∞———

Q. Where is Maine's largest gem and mineral show?

A. Portland, each June.

———∞∞∞———

Q. Where did the cast and crew of the Twentieth Century-Fox film *Deep Waters* stay during the making of the movie in 1947?

A. Hotel Rockland on the corner of Rockland's Main and Park Streets.

———∞∞∞———

Q. What town is known as the leader in the frozen custard world?

A. New Gloucester, home of Hyacinth Hodgman's frozen custard stand.

———∞∞∞———

Q. How long has the Hi-Hat Pancake House in Farmingdale been in business?

A. Since 1944.

———∞∞∞———

Q. What dessert has made Helen's Restaurant in Machias famous?

A. Homemade strawberry pie.

Q. What was Rudy Vallee's theme song?

A. "My Time Is Your Time."

Q. How many passengers can board the sightseeing vessel *Voyageur* out of Belfast, Maine?

A. 150. (Sightings of seals are common.)

Q. What are the Bay Chamber Concerts?

A. Weekly concerts at the Rockport Opera House every Thursday night (and some Fridays) during July and August.

Q. Where is the Fishermen's Museum?

A. Pemaquid Point Lighthouse keeper's cottage, at the end of Route 130 in Pemaquid Point.

Q. Who was known as "the Dean of American Composers"?

A. John Knowles Paine, a student of Herman Kotzschmar's in Portland.

Q. How was Gardiner's A-1 Diner billed when it opened in 1946?

A. "Maine's Most Modernistic Diner."

Q. Who plays at Kennebunk's Concert on the Green, in July?

A. The Casco Bay Concert Band.

Q. What entertainment was offered at the Acme Pavilion in Winthrop in 1912?

A. Bowling, billiards, and movies.

Q. How did the Fat Boy Drive-In in Brunswick get its name when it opened in 1955?

A. Founder John Bollinger had seen the name on a California drive-in.

Q. Who designed the Portland Theater, opened as a vaudeville theater in 1909?

A. Boston architect Henri Desmond.

Q. What was Maine's first open-air movie theater?

A. Saco Drive-In, opened in the summer of 1939.

Q. What was the opening vaudeville act at the Portland Theater?

A. H. C. Wilson's Bears, Dogs, and Ant Eaters.

Q. What is Hollywood director John Ford's real name?

A. Sean Aloysius O'Feeny, born in Portland in 1896.

Q. What Maine radio station was known as "the powerhouse popular music station" during the early 1960s?

A. Portland station WLOB.

Q. The first French language programs were broadcast by what Maine radio station?

A. WCOU of Lewiston, in the 1940s.

———⊂⊃⊃⊃———

Q. When did film actor Anthony Quinn visit Maine?

A. June 1945, to promote his movie *Return to Bataan.*

———⊂⊃⊃⊃———

Q. What was the first Maine diner to install a cigarette vending machine?

A. Jack's Lunch, in Bath, in 1934.

———⊂⊃⊃⊃———

Q. What was the entertainment menu at the Island Ledge Casino on Wells Beach when it opened in 1909?

A. Dancing Tuesday, Thursday, and Saturday nights; movies on the other evenings.

———⊂⊃⊃⊃———

Q. Who established the first television station in New England?

A. Thompson L. Guernsey of Dover-Foxcroft, in 1940, when he started operating television station WIXG-TV, Channel 1, Boston.

———⊂⊃⊃⊃———

Q. What is the oldest continuously broadcast religious radio program in the nation?

A. *The First Radio Parish Church of America,* which premiered on WCSH radio in Portland in 1926.

———⊂⊃⊃⊃———

Q. Where in Maine is the Italian Street Festival?

A. Portland, in August.

Q. How old is Rockland's Strand Theater?

A. Seventy-five years, as of February 21, 1998.

Q. What is the real name of the Humble Farmer, the well-known Maine storyteller?

A. Robert Skoglund.

Q. Jazz clarinetist Brad Terry gets his mail at what location?

A. Macbean's Music on Brunswick's Maine Street.

Q. How much was the price of admission to hear Benny Goodman and his orchestra at Old Orchard Beach Pier in 1938?

A. One dollar.

Q. Where are the Maine Highland Games held each August?

A. Thomas Point Beach, in Brunswick.

Q. Where is the Piscataquis Valley Fair held each August?

A. The fairgrounds in Dover-Foxcroft.

Q. How many artists exhibit in the Ogunquit Annual Sidewalk Art Show?

A. About eighty.

Q. What are the Logging Museum Festival Days?

A. An annual event held in Rangeley every July.

Q. What Portland dancer was in the movie *Carousel*?

A. Jacques D'Amboise, who danced in the ballet scene.

Q. One of the nation's oldest summer theaters is in what town?

A. Ogunquit, home of the Ogunquit Playhouse.

Q. Where can you enjoy a display of vintage autos?

A. Wells Auto Museum in Wells.

Q. The movie *Captains Courageous* was filmed in what town in 1937?

A. Camden was the locale for Kipling's tale of fishing off the Grand Banks.

Q. Who is Miss Dumpy?

A. Queen of the annual Kennebunkport Dump Pageant.

Q. Where is the Maine Festival of the Arts staged each year?

A. Brunswick.

Q. What food product is associated with an annual festival in Yarmouth?

A. Clams.

Q. Where was *Emmeline* filmed?

A. Fayette.

Q. What positions did Sean O'Feeny (John Ford) play on the Portland High School football team?

A. Running back and defensive lineman.

Q. Where is Maine's annual teddy bear show?

A. Kennebearport, every August.

Q. Where is radio station WCXX-FM located?

A. Madawaska.

Q. Who owns radio station WZON-AM in Bangor?

A. Best-selling author Stephen King, who lives in Bangor.

Q. How large was the screen on the first television receiver, invented by Thompson Guernsey of Dover-Foxcroft in the early 1940s?

A. One and a half inches in diameter.

Q. When were Maine listeners first introduced to *Morning Pro Musica* on National Public Radio?

A. 1941.

Q. In what month is the annual Skowhegan State Fair held?

A. August.

Q. Where is Maine's longest bathing beach?

A. Old Orchard Beach. It's seven miles long.

Q. How long is the amusement park that borders Old Orchard Beach?

A. Almost seven miles.

Q. What was Bette Davis's last film?

A. *The Whales of August,* filmed on Casco Bay.

Q. Where can a Maine visitor find a working colonial kitchen?

A. York Institute in Saco.

Q. Where can a penny candy fan still buy penny candy that still costs a penny?

A. The village of Willowbrook, at Newfield in western York County.

Q. What is special about the Museum at Willowbrook?

A. It features a collection of more than sixty carriages and horse-drawn sleighs.

Q. What Maine town was used as the setting for the TV version of *Peyton Place*?

A. Camden.

Q. Where is Maine's "Outlet Mecca"?

A. Freeport.

Q. In what part of Maine is the Jones Museum of Glass and Ceramics?

A. The rolling hills west of Sebago Lake.

Q. Where can a person dine and hear opera arias and show tunes sung during dinner?

A. Quisiana, a rustic lakeside lodge in Kezar Falls.

Q. What was the Dog House?

A. A popular hot-dog stand in East Hamden, opened in 1936.

Q. "Eat Here and Grow Fat" was the advertisement for what restaurant?

A. Dan Long's Restaurant, in Lewiston, in 1908.

Q. Where is the annual Maine Morgan Horse Show held?

A. Bangor, in August.

Q. Where is the Annual Transportation and Air Show held?

A. Owls Head, in August.

Q. Who wrote the song "Where the Roses Twine the Trellis by the Door"?

A. Harry Augustus Dinsmore, of Skowhegan.

Q. As of May 1998, how long had Portland's Deering Ice Cream Company been in business?

A. 112 years.

Q. What seafood restaurant is at 6 Custom House Wharf in Portland?

A. Boone's, "On the Waterfront Since 1898" as its slogan once claimed.

Q. Who are some of the guests who once registered at the Bangor House?

A. Bette Davis, Paul Whiteman, Jack Benny, Gene Autry, Tommy Dorsey, Duke Ellington, Henry Fonda, and six U.S. presidents.

Q. What does everyone wear in the Chester Greenwood Day parade in downtown Farmington?

A. Earmuffs, in honor of their inventor.

Q. What entertainment was featured at Auto Rest Park in Carmel in 1925?

A. Animal farm, penny arcade, amusement rides, dance hall, and roller-skating rink.

Q. How many Academy Awards did Maine's John Ford win?

A. Four.

Q. What happens on Wings of Winter Day in Belfast Harbor?

A. Bird watchers gather for a field trip to observe wintering birds.

Q. What is the Festival of Lights?

A. An annual Christmas Season event in Eastport, featuring a parade of lighted boats in the harbor.

Q. What is Maine Maple Sunday?

A. A March celebration of spring in Camden, featuring tours of sap houses, tree tapping, and syrup tasting.

Q. Where is the Maine Antique Paper Show?

A. Italian Heritage Center in Portland.

Q. What's to see at a paper show?

A. Antique maps, trade cards, movie posters, catalogs, vintage posters, and more.

Q. What Maine town celebrates a Sparkle Weekend in early December?

A. Freeport.

Q. What was the name of the movie theater in Kingfield from 1925 to 1935?

A. New Kingfield Theater, owned by Hutchinson and Huse.

Q. When were the first outboard motors used to power sightseeing boats on Maine lakes?

A. 1923.

Q. Where was the Dreamland Theater?

A. Livermore Falls, from 1909 until 1961.

Q. Who was Victoria Crandall?

A. Founder of the Maine State Music Theater in Brunswick (founded in 1959).

Q. Where is the world's largest lobster feed?

A. The annual Maine Seafood Festival, in Rockland.

Q. What was the first Maine restaurant with all-electric cooking?

A. Barjo's in Norway, electrified in 1946.

Q. When did the Augusta House open?

A. December 31, 1831, a few weeks before the Maine legislature convened for its first session in the new capital.

Q. What diner is known as Maine's most famous roadside delight?

A. Moody's Diner on Route 1 in Waldoboro.

Q. Moviegoers find popcorn soaked in real butter at what venue?

A. Railroad Cinema and Square Cafe, in Waterville.

Q. Where in Maine is a bed and breakfast with its own built-in sauna?

A. Richmond, on Route 197 (a dirt road). It's called Richmond Corners Sauna and Bed and Breakfast.

Q. Where is the world's largest lobster pot?

A. Rockland, under a huge tent at the public landing.

Q. When are the Bay Chamber Concerts held?

A. Each Thursday evening in July and August, at the Rockport Opera House.

Q. How long is the average windjammer cruise aboard one of Maine's many tall-masted sailing ships?

A. Six days and nights.

Q. The blessing of the fishing fleet in Boothbay Harbor is held when?

A. Early April.

Q. As of December 1997, how many years had Lou McNally hosted *Made in Maine* on public television?

A. Ten.

Q. Who presides at the celebration that follows the annual blessing of the fleet in Boothbay Harbor?

A. The Shrimp Princess.

Q. What Maine jazz group recorded the album *On the Rocks*?

A. Trombonist Don Doane and his band.

Q. Which Maine storyteller appears regularly on the CBS-TV show *Sunday Morning*?

A. Tim Sample.

Q. Where can you watch Maine's largest night parade?

A. The Ossipee Valley Fair, in South Hiram.

Q. When is Maine's Annual Blue Grass Festival?

A. Early September, at Thomas Point Beach.

Q. How old was the Biddeford City Theater in 1996?

A. One hundred years.

⊷∞⊷

Q. What movie about a football star was shown at the Biddeford City Theater in 1926?

A. *One Minute to Play.*

⊷∞⊷

Q. Brunswick's Fat Boy Drive-In holds its annual Sock Hop on what day?

A. The second Saturday in August.

⊷∞⊷

Q. What single attraction draws the largest crowds in Maine?

A. The Blue Angels, the navy's precision flying team, at the annual Brunswick Naval Air Station Air Show.

⊷∞⊷

Q. How long has the Chick-A-Dee Restaurant been on Route 4 in Turner?

A. Since 1936.

⊷∞⊷

Q. How many seats are in the Biddeford City Theater, a National Historic Landmark?

A. 684.

⊷∞⊷

Q. The annual Old Time Fiddler's Contest in Rangeley is held about a week before what event?

A. The Logging Museum Festival.

Q. Maine radio and TV weatherman Lou McNally has what nickname?

A. Altitude Lou.

Q. Who picketed a Falmouth bookstore in 1985, urging patrons not to buy a book by the daughter of his ex-wife?

A. Actor Gary Merrill, former husband of Bette Davis.

Q. Where is Maine's Annual Rockhound Roundup held?

A. Portland, in June.

Q. When did Hildreth Broadcasting build Studio City?

A. May 1962, at the corner of Hildreth and Rice Streets in Bangor.

Q. Who founded the Maine Festival?

A. Marshall Dodge, of *Bert and I* fame.

Q. What stars have made personal appearances at the Biddeford City Theater?

A. Charlie Chaplin, Al Jolson, W. C. Fields, Abbott and Costello, Fred Astaire, and Roy Rogers and his trusty horse Trigger.

Q. What Maine humorist wrote stories that were favorites of President Abraham Lincoln's?

A. Charles Farrar Browne of Waterford, who used the pen name Artemus Ward.

Q. When was the first "talking" picture, *The Jazz Singer,* first shown in Maine?

A. February 1928, at Portland's Empire Theater.

Q. Where was the first Maine Festival?

A. Bowdoin College campus in Brunswick, in 1971.

Q. What was generally regarded as New England's finest drive-in movie theater?

A. Augusta Drive-In Theater in Manchester.

Q. Who recorded *Father Fell Down the Well and Other Maine Stories*?

A. Stephen Evans Merrill, of Skowhegan and Brunswick.

Q. What comedian who appeared on TV's *Rowan and Martin's Laugh-In* lived in Eustis?

A. Justin (Jud) Strunk.

Q. In 1921 Augusta's Holman Day made how many two-reel movies?

A. Twenty-six (one twenty-minute black-and-white movie every two weeks).

Q. What happens in Oxford in late July?

A. The Rotary Club Bean Hole Bean Festival.

Q. Where was humorist Bill Nye born?

A. Shirley Mills, near Moosehead Lake, in 1850.

Q. The Mel Gibson–directed movie *The Man without a Face* was filmed in what town?

A. Camden.

Q. What well-known country-western singer was born in Maine?

A. Dick Curless.

Q. Where is the Acadia Repertory Theater?

A. Somesville, Mount Desert Island.

Q. What Maine lumberjack balladeer composed and sang the popular song "The Grand Trunk Wreck" at the turn of the century?

A. Joe Scott.

Q. What Maine trio is known for singing sea chanteys?

A. Schooner Fare.

Q. Where is the Saint Philip's Chowder Supper held?

A. Wiscasset, on Mondays in July.

Q. What American humorist was born in Buckfield?

A. Seba Smith, in 1792.

Q. The star of a children's hour on Portland's WGME-TV was what Broadway actor?

A. "Captain" Lloyd Knight.

Q. What is the name of the popular quiz show on Maine Public Television?

A. *So You Think You Know Maine.*

Q. What Bangor building was billed as "the finest establishment of its kind in America"?

A. The Bowlodrome, so advertised in 1916.

Q. Who directed and produced the popular Maine Public Television series *Housewarming* in 1976?

A. Angus King, elected Maine's governor in 1994.

Q. Where are the Maine State Music Theater performances?

A. Pickard Theater on the Bowdoin College campus.

Q. Waterville's Vaughan Meador impersonated what prominent American many times on network TV?

A. President John F. Kennedy.

Q. What Maine community celebrates Strawberry Shortcake Day?

A. Presque Isle, in late June.

Q. What folk trio specializes in songs of the sea and Maine?

A. Schoonerfare.

HISTORY

C H A P T E R T H R E E

Q. Who was Maine's first Irish governor?

A. Edward Kavanagh, who served 1843–1844.

Q. The state's only trial for blasphemy was held in what place?

A. South Paris, in 1919.

Q. Who invented the snowplow?

A. Don A. Sargent, of Bangor.

Q. When was Dennysville settled?

A. 1786.

Q. How much snow fell on Caribou in the winter of 1954–55?

A. 181.1 inches, the most since record-keeping began.

Q. For whom was the Dennys River named?

A. A Native-American chief named Denny, who caught Atlantic salmon there.

Q. When did the first McDonald's open in Maine?

A. May 1963, on Saint John Street in Portland.

Q. What does the Native-American word *Abenaki* mean?

A. "People of the dawnland."

Q. When was Millinocket, "the Magic City of the North," founded?

A. 1900.

Q. How many descendants of the original Abenaki still live in Maine?

A. About four thousand.

Q. Where did the first naval battle of the American Revolution take place?

A. Machias Harbor, on May 9, 1775.

Q. For whom was Waldoboro named?

A. Gen. Samuel Waldo, who signed up a group of two hundred German immigrants in 1748, promising them schools and houses if they would settle the town.

Q. Why was Millinocket established?

A. New York developer Garret Schenck decided it would be a perfect site for a paper mill.

———— ∞∞∞ ————

Q. What were the names of the first English ships to land near the mouth of the Kennebec River on May 13, 1607?

A. *Gift of God,* commanded by George Popham; and *Mary and John,* commanded by Raleigh Gilbert.

———— ∞∞∞ ————

Q. What was the verdict in Maine's only trial for blasphemy?

A. Defendant Michael X. Mockus was ruled guilty of words "uttered contumeliously, in a blasphemous manner."

———— ∞∞∞ ————

Q. When was Fort Popham built?

A. 1607.

———— ∞∞∞ ————

Q. What did Capt. John Smith bring back from his exploration of the Maine coast in 1608?

A. Ten thousand beaver skins.

———— ∞∞∞ ————

Q. Who was the first American to be knighted?

A. Sir William Phipps, the son of a farmer who lived near the mouth of the Kennebec River. He was knighted in the early 1600s.

———— ∞∞∞ ————

Q. What does the Native-American name *Androscoggin* mean?

A. "Place where fish are cured."

Q. Who invented the microwave oven?

A. Percy LeBaron Spencer, of Howland, in 1946.

Q. How many Native Americans inhabited Maine in 1614?

A. A little fewer than forty thousand, according to Capt. John Smith.

Q. Which white explorer married a Maine Native American?

A. Baron Castine, who married a chief's daughter. A coastal town still bears his name.

Q. What's a rune stone?

A. A rock slab with chiseled runic (alphabetic) markings, believed left on Maine's coast by Leif Eriksson around the year 1000.

Q. What nationality was English explorer Capt. John Cabot?

A. Italian. His birth name was Giovanni Caboto.

Q. When was Maine's first sawmill built?

A. 1634, near a waterfall in South Berwick.

Q. Maine abolished the death penalty in what year?

A. 1876, following the hanging of John True Gordon, later found to be innocent.

Q. What was the name of the British warship that fought in the Revolutionary naval battle in Machias Harbor?

A. *Margaretta.*

Q. Where was Nelson Rockefeller born?

A. Bar Harbor, in 1908.

Q. Where was the first French Jesuit mission in North America?

A. Mount Desert Island, established in 1613.

Q. Who built the Portland Observatory?

A. Capt. Lemuel Moody, in 1807.

Q. What Skowhegan native was the first woman elected to the U.S. Senate?

A. Margaret Chase Smith, in 1949.

Q. Who perfected the seedless orange?

A. Luther Calvin Tibbetts, born in South Berwick.

Q. Who was the only Maine Native American ever to be knighted?

A. Nescambious, for his bravery during the French and Indian War.

Q. What were Maine's popular-vote results in the 1960 presidential election?

A. Nixon, 240,608; Kennedy, 181,159.

Q. What is the oldest European artifact ever discovered in Maine?

A. A small penny, unearthed at Blue Hill in the 1970s and believed minted in Norway between 1066 and 1068.

Q. When did Maine become a state?

A. March 15, 1820.

Q. How far could the longest-range cannon at Fort Knox shoot?

A. More than two miles, the range of the Rodman cannon.

Q. Who wrote the education sections of Maine's constitution?

A. Thomas Jefferson.

Q. Who was the nation's first secretary of war?

A. Gen. Henry Knox, of Thomaston.

Q. What Maine structure is one of the oldest English public buildings surviving in North America?

A. The Old Gaol in York, built in 1719.

Q. What is Maine's oldest town?

A. Kittery, incorporated in 1652.

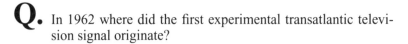

Q. Where is the oldest surviving original blockhouse in the nation?

A. Winslow, Fort Halifax, built in 1754.

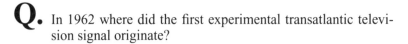

Q. What is most remembered about Maine's Fort William Henry in Bristol?

A. It was captured by every force that ever attacked it.

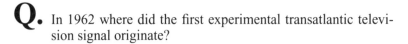

Q. Why is "Lovewell's Fight" still remembered?

A. Joseph Lovewell's band of rangers defeated the Native-American Sokokis at Fryeburg in 1725.

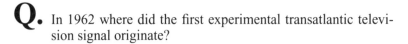

Q. In 1962 where did the first experimental transatlantic television signal originate?

A. Andover, the site of Bell Telephone's Telstar Earth Station.

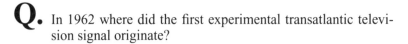

Q. In 1804 who led a task force against the Barbary pirates of Tripoli?

A. Com. Edward Preble, of Falmouth.

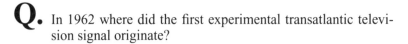

Q. For whom is the town of Orono named?

A. Penobscot Chief Joseph Orono, the blond-haired, blue-eyed Native American who helped George Washington during the American Revolution.

Q. Approximately how old was Penobscot Chief Joseph Orono when he died?

A. More than one hundred years.

———

Q. Who is Kittery's most famous native son?

A. Sir William Pepperell, who in 1745 captured the French fort at Louisbourg, Nova Scotia, one of the major events of the French and Indian Wars.

———

Q. Civil War Gen. Oliver Otis Howard, a Leeds native, is best remembered for what postwar achievement?

A. Founding Howard University.

———

Q. How much did a Maine driver's license cost in 1905?

A. Two dollars.

———

Q. What is the Lafayette Elm in Kennebunk?

A. The tree under which the Marquis de Lafayette stood during his trip to Maine in 1825.

———

Q. When was Fort George built at Castine?

A. 1779.

———

Q. Who founded Maine's Republican Party?

A. William Pitt Fessenden, during the early 1850s.

Q. Whose was the first name drawn in the national draft during the Civil War?

A. Edward Francis White's, of Portland.

Q. Who was Maine's governor just after the Civil War?

A. Gen. Joshua L. Chamberlain, the hero of the battle of Little Round Top at Gettysburg.

Q. How many Portland streets are named after William Pitt Fessenden?

A. Three: William Street, Pitt Street, and Fessenden Street.

Q. Under whose direct command were the Confederate troops defeated by Chamberlain's Twentieth Maine troops at Gettysburg?

A. Confederate Gen. James Longstreet.

Q. What was the nation's first city to adopt military training in its public schools?

A. Bangor, in 1862.

Q. Where was President Jimmy Carter's secretary of state and former senator Edmund S. Muskie born?

A. Rumford.

Q. What delicacy was served to the Marquis de Lafayette when he visited Maine in 1825?

A. Ice cream.

Q. When was the first Maine state-approved lottery?

A. 1823, conducted by the Cumberland and Oxford Canal Corporation.

———∞———

Q. What was historic about the train trip to Canton made by the Portland and Oxford Central Railroad?

A. The train traveled across tracks laid on the frozen surface of Canton Lake.

———∞———

Q. What became of the tracks the Portland and Oxford Central Railroad laid across the ice?

A. They sank in the spring when the ice melted.

———∞———

Q. How did the British colonists identify the Maine white pines selected for use as masts by the English Royal Navy?

A. They marked each tree with a painted arrowhead, pointing upward.

———∞———

Q. What is the inscription on Chief Joseph Orono's tombstone?

A. "Safe lodged within his blanket below . . . Lie the last relics of old Orono."

———∞———

Q. What mayor of Portland ran for U.S. president on the Prohibition Party ticket?

A. Neal Dow, in 1880.

———∞———

Q. Who was the highest-ranking woman in the U.S. Marine Corps in 1971?

A. Col. Hazel E. Benn, of Smyrna Mills.

Q. When was Machias settled?

A. 1633.

Q. How large did a Maine white pine need to be for naval use?

A. Two feet in diameter, measured a foot from the ground.

Q. Who designed Maine's capitol in Augusta?

A. Charles Bulfinch, who also served as architect for the Capitol in Washington, D.C.

Q. Where did President Lyndon Johnson stop for a roadside snack during his Maine visit in 1964?

A. The Topsham Dairy Queen (the phrase "Lyndon Johnson ate here" is still painted on the stand's exterior).

Q. What did U.S. Sen. Margaret Chase Smith wear each day in the Senate?

A. A fresh red rose.

Q. When was Ed Muskie first elected governor of Maine?

A. 1954, on the Democratic ticket.

Q. In Maine in the eighteenth century, how many times a week could you feed lobster to your servants?

A. Three.

Q. Who was Boss Reed?

A. Thomas Brackett Reed, of Portland, Speaker of the U.S. House of Representatives, 1895–1899.

Q. When did Benedict Arnold lead a successful march through Maine to Quebec?

A. 1775. (This expedition made him a hero of the Revolution before he turned traitor.)

Q. Why were Americans exhorted to "Remember the Maine!" in 1898?

A. The U.S. battleship *Maine* was blown up in Havana Harbor, starting the Spanish-American War.

Q. What year was the Great Portland Fire?

A. 1866.

Q. Where is the oldest pile bridge in America?

A. York, built in 1761.

Q. In what year did Maine colonists celebrate their first Thanksgiving?

A. 1607.

Q. Maine is the only state in the nation with the facilities to do what with sardines?

A. Can and pack them.

Q. When was the first sardine cannery built in Eastport?

A. 1876.

Q. Who led an entire American fleet to defeat in 1779?

A. Com. Dudley Saltonstall, whose expedition of nineteen armed ships and twenty-four transports was defeated by the British in the Penobscot River.

Q. What are Reed's Rules?

A. Parliamentary guidelines established by Speaker Reed that are still in use in the Maine legislature.

Q. Where did the Maine Republican Party hold its first organized convention?

A. Strong, on August 7, 1854.

Q. When did the National Grange of the Patrons of Husbandry first come to Maine?

A. 1873.

Q. What happened to Commodore Saltonstall after his defeat by the British in 1779?

A. He was tried in military court, found guilty, and court-martialed.

Q. When was Maine's worst forest fire?

A. October 1947, when much of Bar Harbor was burned to the ground.

Q. Whom did Grover Cleveland defeat when he ran for president in 1884?

A. Republican James G. Blaine, of Maine.

———⊗———

Q. What document permanently established the Maine-Canada boundary?

A. The Webster-Ashburton Treaty of 1842.

———⊗———

Q. How many Maine men served the Union army during the Civil War?

A. About seventy-three thousand.

———⊗———

Q. Whom did President Lincoln call "the little lady who started the big war"?

A. Harriet Beecher Stowe, who wrote *Uncle Tom's Cabin* while she lived in Brunswick.

———⊗———

Q. When did Maine's population pass the one-million mark?

A. 1971.

———⊗———

Q. Where was Maine's first State House?

A. Congress Street in Portland, the capital from 1820 to 1833.

———⊗———

Q. Whom did Gen. Ulysses S. Grant name to receive the formal stacking of arms of Gen. Robert E. Lee's men at Appomattox?

A. Gen. Joshua Chamberlain.

Q. When were the first prisoners jailed in the Maine State Prison?

A. 1824, when the facility opened in Thomaston.

Q. Who was Maine's first Independent governor?

A. James B. Longley, elected in 1974.

Q. Who commanded the first torpedo boat flotilla in the Spanish-American War?

A. Rear Adm. William Kimball, a Maine native.

Q. Who were the first two women in the nation to cast ballots in a national contest?

A. Gertrude Southard, of Bangor, and Alice Skolfield, of Lewiston.

Q. Who was the candidate when Maine voted for its first Democratic Party presidential candidate in fifty-two years?

A. Lyndon Johnson, election of 1964.

Q. What did James Longley do more than any other Maine governor?

A. He vetoed 109 bills.

Q. What two Native-American tribes still survive in Maine?

A. Penobscot and Passamaquoddy.

Q. Who became known as the nation's "Father of Prohibition"?

A. Neal Dow.

Q. In what year did the first Republican begin his term as the Maine governor?

A. 1855, Anson P. Morillo.

Q. Until 1960 why did Maine hold its elections for Congress and governor in September?

A. It was thought November's bad weather would keep too many voters from the polls.

Q. What nineteenth-century Maine congressman was killed in a duel?

A. Jonathan Cilley, shot by U.S. Representative William Graves of Kentucky.

Q. How old was Maine governor Edmund Muskie when he took the oath of office in 1955?

A. Forty.

Q. When was the University of Maine established?

A. 1865, at Orono.

Q. How many Maine troops died in World War II?

A. 1,634 of the 80,000 who served.

Q. Which Augusta native served as Chief Justice of the U.S. Supreme Court?

A. Melville W. Fuller, served 1888–1910.

―――∞∞∞―――

Q. Who started America's gum-chewing habit?

A. John Curtis, a Maine seaman, who began manufacturing State of Maine Pure Spruce Gum in 1848.

―――∞∞∞―――

Q. Who served as U.S. attorney general from 1846 to 1848?

A. Nathan Clifford, of Newfield.

―――∞∞∞―――

Q. When did French statesman Charles Maurice de Talleyrand visit Maine?

A. 1794.

―――∞∞∞―――

Q. How many militiamen did Gov. Thomas Pownall lead up the Penobscot River in May 1759?

A. Four hundred.

―――∞∞∞―――

Q. Who is known as "the Father of the Maine Railroads"?

A. John A. Poor, of West Andover, who established the Montreal-to-Portland line.

―――∞∞∞―――

Q. How many destroyers were built for the U.S. Navy at Maine's Bath Iron Works during World War II?

A. Eighty-two.

Q. What community bills itself as "Maine's Prettiest Village"?

A. Wiscasset, on the banks of the Sheepscot River.

Q. From what country did the first cattle to land in Maine arrive?

A. Denmark, in 1634.

Q. Who invented the first steam-powered threshing machine?

A. Hiram and John Pitts, of Winthrop.

Q. What popular toothpaste is made in Maine?

A. Tom's of Maine.

Q. What museum contains the world's largest collection of streetcars?

A. Seacoast Trolley Museum in Kennebunkport, founded in 1939.

Q. Who invented the steam log hauler?

A. Alvin O. Lombard, of Waterville, in 1901.

Q. How many Liberty Ships were built in South Portland during World War II?

A. 236.

Q. What was one of the port of Portland's most profitable nineteenth-century imports?

A. Rum from the West Indies.

Q. Where is the Peary-MacMillan Arctic Museum?

A. Bowdoin College, in Brunswick.

Q. Who drove a Stanley Steamer automobile to the top of Mount Washington in 1902?

A. Freelon Stanley and his wife.

Q. What was the first newspaper published in Maine?

A. The *Falmouth Gazette,* printed in Portland on January 1, 1785.

Q. Where is the oldest naval shipyard in the nation?

A. Kittery.

Q. Where was Judge Crater's home when he vanished in 1930?

A. Belgrade.

Q. Who was the first woman ever to have her name placed in nomination for U.S. president by a major political party?

A. Sen. Margaret Chase Smith, in 1964 (she lost the Republican nomination to Sen. Barry Goldwater).

Q. What are the livelihoods of the two men pictured on the Maine State Seal?

A. The one on the left is a farmer; the other is a mariner.

Q. What is Maine's official state animal?

A. The moose.

Q. Who were the first Native Americans to be granted the right of representation in the Maine legislature?

A. The Penobscot Native Americans of Old Town, on October 11, 1786.

Q. From the founding of the Republic until Maine became a state, what was its official status?

A. Part of the state of Massachusetts.

Q. When was the eight-hour work day first enacted into law?

A. July 3, 1794, in Camden.

Q. What was Maine's first antislavery newspaper?

A. The *Advocate of Freedom,* first published in Hallowell in 1838.

Q. How much did Gen. Peleg Washburn pay for seventy-eight hundred acres of Maine land in 1787?

A. A bit less than a thousand dollars.

Q. When did school attendance first become compulsory for Maine children?

A. 1875 (the law required children ages nine to fifteen to attend school for at least twelve weeks per year).

Q. In 1796 what did Paul Coffin say about the road from Otisfield to Bethel?

A. It was "rocky, rooty, muddy, and truly bad."

Q. What happened to the boy Daniel Eaton, of Brunswick, when he was captured by Native Americans in 1757?

A. He was taken to Canada and sold for four dollars.

Q. Who published Maine's first newspaper, the *Falmouth Gazette*?

A. Benjamin Titcomb Jr. and Thomas B. Wait.

Q. How many new ships were launched in Searsport between 1770 and 1920?

A. More than three thousand.

Q. Who made the sleds used by Arctic explorer Donald MacMillan?

A. Henry Franklin Morton, founder of the Paris Manufacturing Company in Paris, in 1860.

Q. In what year did Maine experience a frost every month?

A. 1816, known as "Eighteen-hundred-and-froze-to-death."

Q. What is the source of the quotation, "As Maine goes, so goes the nation"?

A. For many years, in its September local elections, Maine voters often chose candidates from the party that won the November elections in other states.

Q. What naval commander is said to have sunk every ship he ever engaged?

A. Com. Edward Preble, of Portland, 1761–1807.

Q. Where was Maine's first medical school?

A. Bowdoin College, in Brunswick, opened in 1820.

Q. How many blacksmith shops were in Maine in 1856?

A. 974, about two for every town and village.

Q. Where were toothpicks invented?

A. In Maine, by Charles Forster of Bangor, soon after the Civil War.

Q. What is New England's second-oldest agricultural newspaper?

A. The *Maine Farmer,* first published in 1833 by Ezekiel Holmes, also its editor.

Q. When was the Maine Board of Agriculture founded?

A. 1857, to encourage farmers to modernize and upgrade.

Q. How many operating sawmills were counted in Maine in 1682?

A. Twenty-four, six of them in Kittery.

Q. On what ship was a cargo of granite shipped from Vinalhaven to Boston in 1829?

A. *Plymouth Rock.*

Q. When was the last log drive on a Maine river?

A. 1975, on the Kennebec.

Q. When was the last covered bridge built in Maine?

A. 1911, the Watson Settlement Covered Bridge, five miles north of Houlton.

Q. How many tins of sardines were packed each year at the canneries in Lubec during the first half of the twentieth century?

A. About 120 million.

Q. How did Sen. Edmund S. Muskie's father, Steven, make a living?

A. He was a tailor, in Rumford.

Q. During the 1850s, what was the world's busiest lumber port?

A. Bangor.

Q. Where did the townspeople of Machias make plans to attack the British schooner *Margaretta* anchored in the harbor in 1770?

A. Burnham Tavern.

Q. What is the Thomas Hill Standpipe?

A. A shingled Bangor water tower built of wood, 110 feet tall, with an observation deck.

Q. When was the first wood pulp produced in Maine?

A. 1868, marking the start of what is now the state's largest industry—pulp and paper.

Q. When did Maine enact a law prohibiting compulsory retirement at sixty-five?

A. 1977, the first state to do so.

Q. When did Maine's state colleges unite to become the University of Maine?

A. 1968.

Q. How many ship's captains lived in Searsport during the 1800s?

A. 286.

Q. What is a Queen Atlantic?

A. A massive kitchen stove manufactured by the Portland Foundry.

Q. What Maine community was the staging point for Benedict Arnold's expeditionary force assembled to attack Quebec in 1775?

A. Gardiner, on the banks of the Kennebec River.

⸺∞⸺

Q. When were the first female students admitted to Colby College in Waterville?

A. 1871.

⸺∞⸺

Q. What is the largest wooden ship ever built in America?

A. The 392-foot *Wyoming,* built at the Percy and Small shipyard on the banks of the Kennebec River and launched in 1909.

⸺∞⸺

Q. Where is the only remaining pre-Revolutionary courthouse in Maine?

A. Pownalborough Court House, built in 1752 on the Fort Shirley parade grounds.

⸺∞⸺

Q. What Maine product did American troops find in Manuel Noriega's palace in Panama during the October 1989 military action?

A. A tube of Tom's of Maine toothpaste.

⸺∞⸺

Q. Who produced the first Shirley Temple doll?

A. Herbert A. Brown, of Fairfield, in 1934.

⸺∞⸺

Q. When was Maine's first college founded?

A. 1794, when Bowdoin College opened its doors.

Q. What president sought a safe anchorage at Northeast Harbor on August 15, 1873?

A. President Ulysses S. Grant, whose yacht had encountered a bad summer storm.

Q. What Maine town was one of the last in the nation to use magneto, or "crank," telephones?

A. Bryant Pond, which did not switch to more modern equipment until October 1983.

Q. Where is the last active Shaker community in the nation?

A. Sabbathday Lake.

Q. What is the Strathglass Park Historic District?

A. Fifty-one elegant brick buildings in Rumford, built in 1901 by Hugh Chisholm's Oxford Paper Company in hopes of attracting a qualified work force.

Q. Who made the largest fiberglass flagpoles in the world?

A. Joe and Glenith Grey, of Sargentville, in 1974 and 1975. They were one hundred feet tall and five feet wide at the base.

Q. When was iron ore first discovered in Maine?

A. 1843 at Ore Mountain, by geographer Moses Greenleaf.

Q. For what was Harold Casey of Passadumkeag best known?

A. He was one of the world's greatest taxidermists.

Q. How many telephones were in Portland in 1880?

A. 105.

Q. What Maine town was founded by William W. Thomas of Portland in 1870?

A. New Sweden, northwest of Caribou in Aroostook County.

Q. Who founded the Prudential Insurance Company?

A. John Dryden, of Temple Mills, in 1875.

Q. Who built the nation's first oilcloth factory?

A. Ezekiel J. Bailey, of Winthrop, in 1845.

Q. What college was founded by the Maine Literary and Theological Society in 1813?

A. Colby College, on Mayflower Hill in Waterville.

Q. What was the first lighthouse completed after the founding of the United States and one of the oldest in continuous use in the nation?

A. Portland Head Light, first operated in 1791 on orders of George Washington.

Q. What famous privateer was built at Porter's Landing in Freeport in 1813?

A. The *Dash,* a 222-ton sailing ship said to be the fastest afloat in her day.

Q. Who was Maine's second Independent governor?

A. Angus King, who took office in 1994.

Q. Where were golf tees first produced?

A. Norway, Maine.

Q. What Maine man was knighted by Queen Victoria?

A. Machine-gun inventor Hiram Maxim, of Sangerville, in 1901.

Q. Where was the nation's first white-flour mill?

A. Norway, Maine, during the 1850s.

Q. What was the first warship to fly the Stars and Stripes?

A. *Ranger,* built for Capt. John Paul Jones at Maine's Kittery-Portsmouth shipyard.

Q. When did Southwest Harbor's Claremont Hotel celebrate its one hundredth birthday?

A. August 18, 1984.

Q. How many Maine men and women were licensed pilots in 1936?

A. Twenty-nine.

Q. When did President Franklin Roosevelt sign the bill that created Acadia National Park?

A. November 1941, just weeks before Pearl Harbor.

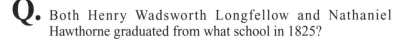

Q. How many carriages were in the Portland parade honoring Lafayette in the summer of 1825?

A. Three.

Q. When were the first telegraph lines strung from Portland to Bangor?

A. 1848.

Q. Both Henry Wadsworth Longfellow and Nathaniel Hawthorne graduated from what school in 1825?

A. Bowdoin College.

Q. Where were the first shoes made in Maine?

A. New Gloucester, in 1850, where shoes were made by hand and hemlock bark was used to tan leather.

Q. When was most of the city of Bangor destroyed by fire?

A. 1911.

Q. What city was home to the nation's oldest city-owned railroad?

A. Belfast, which owned the Belfast and Moosehead Railroad until 1991.

Q. What did Mildred Dunham of Waterville invent in 1936?

A. The Vue-Back Vanity Mirror, which is said to have "sold like hot cakes."

Q. What does a Vue-Back Mirror do?

A. It hooks around the neck and allows free use of the hands.

Q. What was the largest ship ever built at Freeport?

A. The three-masted *John A. Briggs,* built in 1878.

Q. How long has the Cascade Inn been on Route 1 in Saco?

A. Since 1930.

Q. As a student at Bowdoin College, what friend of Nathaniel Hawthorne and Henry Wadsworth Longfellow became fourteenth president of the United States?

A. Franklin Pierce.

ARTS & LITERATURE

C H A P T E R   F O U R

Q. Who was known as the "most popular singer in America" at the turn of the century?

A. Anna "Annie" Louise Cary of Wayne.

Q. Who was the first American to win national fame as a sculptor?

A. Franklin Simmons, born in Portland in 1839.

Q. What composer wrote the first American oratorio *(Saint Peter)*?

A. John Knowles Paine, of Portland, in 1873.

Q. Whose gift established the Ogunquit Museum of Art?

A. Artist Henry Strater's, in 1952.

Q. How tall is the Native-American monument in Skowhegan, sculpted by Bernard Langlais?

A. Sixty feet.

Q. What Maine composer wrote "Sweetheart Sigh No More" in 1918?

A. Emily Peace Meader, a Waterville pianist.

Q. Where was composer Walter Piston born?

A. Rockland, in 1894.

Q. Who sculpted the statue of William Wadsworth Longfellow in Portland's Longfellow Square?

A. Franklin Simmons.

Q. How many paintings a year did Harpswell artist Stephen Etnier finish?

A. Fifty to sixty.

Q. Where was artist Winslow Homer's studio?

A. Prout's Neck.

Q. What orchestra premiered Walter Piston's *Pine Tree Fantasy*?

A. The Portland Symphony Orchestra, in 1965.

Q. Who wrote the march played at John F. Kennedy's funeral?

A. Robert Brown Hall, of Waterville.

Q. What well-known artist lived on 700-Acre Island near Isleboro?

A. Charles Dana Gibson, creator of the Gibson Girl.

Q. Why did Henry Wadsworth Longfellow wear such a full beard?

A. To hide the scars acquired during his unsuccessful attempt to rescue his second wife after she accidentally set her dress on fire at their Portland home.

Q. Where is one of Maine's finest collections of marine paintings?

A. Douglas and Margaret Carver Gallery of the Penobscot Marine Museum.

Q. What was the real name of Farmington soprano Lillian Nordica, who made her American debut at the Metropolitan Opera in 1890?

A. Lillian Norton.

Q. What Maine cornet virtuoso was given a gold-plated cornet in Bangor in 1884?

A. Robert Brown Hall.

Q. Who designed Maine's Haystack Mountain School of the Arts on Jericho Bay?

A. Edward Larrabee Barnes, in the 1960s.

Q. Where is the William A. Farnsworth Art Museum?

A. Rockland.

Q. Where did *Charlotte's Web* author E. B. White spend much of his time?

A. At his farm in Allen Cove.

Q. Which composer was named honorary fire chief of the Hancock (Maine) Volunteer Fire Department?

A. Pierre Monteaux.

Q. Where was poet Edward Arlington Robinson born?

A. Head Tide (in 1869).

Q. What operatic soprano grew up in Bath?

A. Emma Eames.

Q. Where did novelist Stephen King go to college?

A. University of Maine at Orono.

Q. What song composed by Portland composer Harvey S. Murray was sung at the Maine Music Festival in October 1897?

A. "When Richelieu the Red Robe Wore."

Q. What Rockland-born poet was the first woman to win the Pulitzer Prize for poetry?

A. Edna Saint Vincent Millay, in 1923.

Q. Who wrote the song "Old Robin Bids Farewell"?

A. Eugene Francis Johnson, of Portland.

Q. Which two towns claim to be the state's antiques capital?

A. Searsport and Hallowell.

Q. In 1980 what museum exhibited one hundred works of Maine artist Marsden Hartley?

A. New York City's Whitney Museum.

Q. Who wrote the song "I Cannot Spin Tonight"?

A. Ira Cushing Stockbridge, of Freeport.

Q. What Brunswick author wrote the collection of essays titled *In Maine*?

A. John N. Cole.

Q. Where is the world's most photogenic lighthouse?

A. Portland Head Light in Fort Williams Park, Cape Elizabeth (so named because of the number of times it has been painted, photographed, and sketched, and appeared on calendars).

Q. Who wrote "A Salute to Maine"?

A. Daphne Winslow Merrill, of Auburn.

Q. What artist and sculptor was once captain of the Rockland girls basketball team?

A. Louise Nevelson, whose 1958 exhibit at the Museum of Modern Art was termed "extraordinary."

Q. Who wrote the 1888 song "De Water in de Ribber Might Be Wet"?

A. William Grant Brooks, of Saco.

Q. What Georgetown artist is best known for her illustrations of children's books?

A. Dahlov Ipcar.

Q. In 1861 what York resident wrote the melody for the hymn "Jesus Loves Me"?

A. William B. Bradbury.

Q. In the early 1600s what Black Point resident wrote the essays on botany in the book *New England Rarities*?

A. John Josselyn.

Q. What was the title of Fitz Hugh Lane's best-known Maine painting?

A. *Twilight on the Kennebec,* painted in 1860.

Q. What is Maine's largest writers and publishers organization?

A. Maine Writers and Publishers Alliance, in Brunswick.

Q. Who wrote the essay collection *I Begin Through Grass: A Maine Journal*?

A. Alexander Bacon Brook.

Q. After serving as a Civil War battlefield illustrator for *Harper's Weekly,* what world-famous painter of the sea settled permanently at Prout's Neck on the Maine coast?

A. Winslow Homer.

Q. Which Maine island was a particular magnet for painters of the Hudson River School?

A. Mount Desert Island.

Q. Brunswick was the home of what Pulitzer Prize-winning poet?

A. Robert P. Tristam Coffin.

Q. What Pulitzer Prize-winning novelist wrote much of his work on his yacht anchored off Kennebunkport?

A. Booth Tarkington.

Q. Who is considered America's first female novelist?

A. Sarah Sayward Keating Wood of York, in the early nineteenth century.

Q. What was the real name of Artemus Ward, Lincoln's favorite humor writer?

A. Charles Farrar Browne, of Waterford.

Q. Who designed the Great Seal of Maine?

A. Dr. Benjamin Vaughn, of Hallowell.

———⌘———

Q. The hallway walls of what 1813 Bethel home still display their original Rufus Porter murals?

A. Moses Mason House.

———⌘———

Q. Clarence Mulford wrote his Hopalong Cassidy novels in what town?

A. Fryeburg.

———⌘———

Q. Where is the Lillian Nordica Homestead Museum?

A. Off Route 4, two miles north of Farmington.

———⌘———

Q. What fine example of Victorian architecture, now at Poland Springs, was originally built to represent Maine at the 1893 Columbian Exposition in Chicago?

A. Maine State Building.

———⌘———

Q. Who built Portland's Wadsworth-Longfellow house?

A. Gen. Peleg Wadsworth, maternal grandfather of poet Henry Wadsworth Longfellow.

———⌘———

Q. Where can you find one of the nation's largest music box collections?

A. Musical Wonder House in Wiscasset.

Q. What pen name did South Berwick-born novelist and short story writer Sarah Orne Jewett use for her early writings?

A. Alice C. Eliot.

———

Q. What was Nathaniel Hawthorne doing as he wrote the first words of his novel *The Scarlet Letter*?

A. Drifting in a skiff on Sebago Lake.

———

Q. In 1997 what publisher released *Art of the Maine Islands*?

A. Down East Books.

———

Q. Who said, "When I arrive in Maine, I start seeing again"?

A. Painter William Kienbusch.

———

Q. Who wrote *All This and Heaven Too*?

A. Rachel Field, who lived on the Cranberry Islands.

———

Q. The novel of what Maine author became a popular TV soap opera?

A. Gladys Hasty Carroll. *As the Earth Turns* became TV's *As the World Turns*.

———

Q. What Maine music teacher was honored by the emperor of Japan?

A. Luther Whiting Mason, of Turner, who was so honored for introducing the eight-note scale.

Q. Who said, "Never put more than two waves in a painting"?

A. Winslow Homer, of Prout's Neck.

Q. In 1905 artist Rockwell Kent first visited what Maine island?

A. Monhegan.

Q. Who wrote *The Lady of Aroostook*?

A. William Dean Howells, once the editor of *Atlantic Monthly.*

Q. *Icebound* won the Pulitzer Prize for drama in 1923 for what Bangor playwright?

A. Owen Davis.

Q. Where is the Wendell Gilley Gallery?

A. Southwest Harbor. The gallery features more than two hundred bird models by the master woodcarver.

Q. What is novelist Stephen King's favorite pen name?

A. Richard Bachman.

Q. What Blue Hill resident was one of Maine's first notable painters in the late 1700s and early 1800s?

A. Jonathan Fisher.

Q. Which Tony Award nominee once worked for the *Brunswick Record*?

A. Playwright Tina Howe.

Q. Who was the 1996–97 director of the Maine Writers and Publishers Alliance?

A. Paul Doiron.

Q. In 1989 who painted the gouache on paper titled *Islands, Allagash*?

A. Neil Welliver.

Q. Who wrote *The Little Locksmith*?

A. Katherine Butler Hathaway, of Bar Harbor.

Q. What is the title of South Casco author Martin Dibner's most successful book, written in 1953 and made into a movie?

A. *The Deep Sea.*

Q. Where did painter Childe Hassam do much of his work in the 1880s?

A. Appledore Island.

Q. What did painter Neil Welliver say when he first arrived in Maine?

A. "I realized I was in the right place when I hit China Lakes and Palermo."

Q. Sculptor Robert Laurent makes his home in which Maine coast community?

A. Ogunquit.

Q. In 1937 who founded the New England Music Camp at Belgrade Lakes?

A. Dr. Paul Wiggin.

Q. Who composed the well-known "103rd Infantry March"?

A. Arthur Flagg Roundy, of Fairfield.

Q. Who sculpted busts of the men in Lincoln's cabinet?

A. Franklin Simmons, of Portland.

Q. Which state was the first to have a school music project?

A. Maine, in 1966, when Young Audiences, Inc., joined with Music of Maine to provide free live music for school students.

Q. In 1911 who introduced artist George Bellows to Monhegan Island?

A. Artist Rockwell Kent.

Q. What do the initials *E. B.* stand for in E. B. White's name?

A. Elwyn Brooks.

Q. Richard Hooker was the pen name of what Waterville physician who wrote *M.A.S.H.*?

A. Dr. H. Richard Hornberger.

Q. What Rockland-native actress was known as "the Queen of the Stage" in the 1890s?

A. Maxine Elliot (née Jessica Dermott).

Q. What actress once sang "Snappy Syncopaters" with her father's jazz band?

A. Reta Shaw, of South Paris, in the Roaring Twenties.

Q. What mime pupil of Marcel Marceau lives and teaches in South Paris?

A. Tony Montanaro.

Q. Who wrote the historical novel *Come Spring,* about Union, Maine?

A. Ben Ames Williams, who lived in Union.

Q. What Mount Desert Islander was the first woman author in 346 years to be admitted to the Académie Francaise?

A. Marguerite Yourcenar, on March 6, 1980.

Q. Who wrote *The Old Peabody Pew*?

A. Kate Douglas Wiggin, of Hollis Center.

Q. How many books were written by Kennebunkport's Booth Tarkington?

A. Seventy-five.

Q. Where was poet Edna Saint Vincent Millay's Maine summer home?

A. On Ragged Island, in Casco Bay.

Q. Who was known as "the Poet of the Maine Coast"?

A. Wilbert Snow, of Spruce Head.

Q. Who are the members of Maine's "first family" of painting?

A. N. C. Wyeth, Andrew Wyeth, and Jamie Wyeth.

Q. What did Jamie Wyeth tell one art critic about his home on Monhegan?

A. "I could stay right on this point and spend the rest of my life painting."

Q. Who painted *Rangeley October* in 1984?

A. Dahlov Ipcar.

Q. What work of Robert P. Tristram Coffin's won him the 1936 Pulitzer Prize for poetry?

A. *Strange Holiness.*

Q. Which poet wrote more than three hundred verses for greeting cards?

A. Reginald Holmes, of Jay.

———∞∞∞———

Q. Which early Gothic novelist called herself "the Lady of Maine"?

A. Sarah Sayward Keating Wood.

———∞∞∞———

Q. How much money did Harriet Beecher Stowe earn from *Uncle Tom's Cabin* in the first three months after publication?

A. Ten thousand dollars, at that time the largest sum ever earned by an American writer.

———∞∞∞———

Q. When was Sarah Orne Jewett's masterpiece, *The Country of the Pointed Firs,* first published?

A. 1896.

———∞∞∞———

Q. Which artist lives year-round on North Haven Island?

A. Eric Hopkins.

———∞∞∞———

Q. What Maine art school has a nationally renowned summer program?

A. Skowhegan School of Painting and Sculpture.

———∞∞∞———

Q. What woman painted at Maine's York Beach during the 1920s?

A. Georgia O'Keefe.

Q. Who wrote, "Living on an island is about the best way there is left to live"?

A. Robert P. Tristam Coffin, in *Mainstays of Maine,* 1945.

Q. Which well-known painter of Maine seascapes was born in Hawaii?

A. Reuben Tam.

Q. Damariscotta was the retirement place for what Walt Disney illustrator and animator?

A. Maurice "Jake" Day.

Q. When was the Rossini Club of Portland first organized?

A. 1869. It is said to be one of the oldest musical clubs in the nation.

Q. Who composed the "Harvard Hymn"?

A. John Knowles Paine, of Portland, as a tribute to the institution where he was a music professor for forty years.

Q. Where can you find the Maine Women Writers Collection?

A. Westbrook College, in Westbrook.

Q. What series has been called "undoubtedly the most popular series of juvenile books ever published in America"?

A. The Rollo books, by Jacob Abbott, of Brunswick.

Q. Who is called "the father of color photography"?

A. Eliot Porter, who first photographed birds in Maine in 1938.

———⊗≈⊗———

Q. Whom did art critic Edgar Allen Beem call "Maine's most noted portrait artist"?

A. Claude Montgomery, of Portland.

———⊗≈⊗———

Q. What Falmouth resident is the former director of the National Portrait Gallery?

A. Marvin Sadik.

———⊗≈⊗———

Q. Who wrote *Wildfire Loose: The Week Maine Burned*?

A. Joyce Butler, of Kennebunk.

———⊗≈⊗———

Q. What is Maine artist Carlo Pittore's real name?

A. Charles Stanley.

———⊗≈⊗———

Q. Who sculpted the bust of Milton described in Nathaniel Hawthorne's *The Marble Faun*?

A. Westbrook sculptor Paul Akers. The work is now at Colby College.

———⊗≈⊗———

Q. Who is the only American honored by a memorial bust in the Poet's Corner of Westminster Abbey in London?

A. Henry Wadsworth Longfellow, of Portland.

Q. What Maine artist is the leader of Americans for Customary Weight and Measure?

A. Seaver Leslie, of the Morris Farm in Wiscasset.

Q. Which Bowdoinham author illustrated and wrote the 1988 children's book *Trilby's Trumpet*?

A. Sarah Stapler.

Q. What Norway resident was named World Champion of Old Time Fiddlers in 1925?

A. Mellie Dunham.

Q. Who wrote the poem "Last Pine of Sweet Auburn"?

A. Hannah Augusta Moore, born in Wiscasset in 1824.

Q. The children's book *Marmelstein for President* was written in 1978 by whom?

A. Marjorie Weiman Sharmat, of Portland.

Q. Whose landmark photography *As Maine Goes* was exhibited at Bowdoin College in 1968?

A. John McKee.

Q. What Surry resident wrote *The Perfidious Parrot* in 1997?

A. Mystery writer and sculptor Janwillem van de Wetering.

Q. Who founded the Maine Union of Visual Artists?

A. Carlo Pittore.

Q. Who was the first editor (1978) of *Vision,* a journal of the Maine visual arts?

A. Darrah Cole, of North Whitefield.

Q. What was the title of Thomas Cornell's exhibit of paintings at the Bowdoin College Museum of Art in 1990?

A. The Birth of Nature.

Q. Harriet Beecher Stowe wrote what novel set in Maine?

A. *The Pearl of Orr's Island.*

Q. Who received the Deborah Morton Award for Woman of the Year from Westbrook College in 1981?

A. Poet and novelist May Sarton.

Q. Which contemporary Maine painter is best known for his portraits of Maine cities?

A. Robert Solotaire, of Portland.

Q. When did Maine columnist and reporter John Gould write his first novel, *No Other Place*?

A. In 1994, when he was seventy-five.

Q. Who founded the Maine Art Gallery in Wiscasset?

A. Mildred Burrage, in 1957.

Q. What marine artist was born at the Portland Alms House on March 16, 1852?

A. Franklin Stanwood.

Q. Who was named the state poet laureate in 1933?

A. Edna Saint Vincent Millay.

Q. What Skowhegan sculptor created an eight-foot-high metal grasshopper to hold his mailbox?

A. Barry Norling, on Beech Hill Road.

Q. What Hancock artist wrote *The Taste of Color, a Touch of Love,* a book on how to learn to paint?

A. William Moise of Hancock, who self-published his book in 1970.

Q. When did Robert Indiana move to his Vinalhaven studio?

A. 1978.

Q. Which Bowdoinham artist designed the original *Maine Times* in 1968?

A. George Delyra.

Q. What Lewiston attorney has been known as Maine's senior art critic since the late 1960s?

A. Philip Isaacson.

Q. Which Brunswick artist's work was exhibited at the Maine State House three times in the 1970s?

A. Edythe A. Laws.

Q. Who wrote *The Beans of Egypt, Maine*?

A. Carolyn Chute, born in Portland.

Q. How old was Nathaniel Hawthorne when his mother took him to live in Raymond, on the shores of Sebago Lake?

A. Fourteen.

Q. Where was poet Leo Connellan, a three-time Pulitzer nominee, born?

A. Portland. He grew up in Rockland.

Q. Who won the first annual Maine Novel Award in 1986, for *Picking Up*?

A. Linda Honig.

Q. What Maine composer wrote songs for John Denver and Emmylou Harris?

A. Dave Mallett.

Q. Who was the writer-in-residence at the University of Maine in Orono in 1994?

A. Susan Hand Shetterly, of Temple.

Q. Who founded the Maine French Fiddlers in 1987?

A. Donald D. Roy, of Gorham.

Q. Who received a 1996 Maine Arts Commission Traditional Arts Apprenticeship Award for Passamaquoddy (a Native-American tribe) singing and drumming?

A. Delia Mitchell, of Princeton.

Q. What Portland resident won the 1990 Flannery O'Connor Award for Short Fiction?

A. Alfred Depew.

Q. Which calligraphic artist also played string bass with the Bangor Symphony Orchestra in 1996?

A. Jan Owen.

Q. What did Winslow Homer reply when a neighbor asked him why there were so many empty liquor bottles in his Prout's Neck studio?

A. "I don't know, John. I never bought an empty one in my life."

Q. Which Corea artist was hailed by critics in 1917 as "the most accomplished avant-garde artist in America"?

A. Marsden Hartley.

Q. Which Maine artist describes herself as "anarchist in residence"?

A. Abby Shahn, of Solon.

Q. What is the setting for John Greenleaf Whittier's poem "Mogg Megone"?

A. Garrison Cove on Prout's Neck.

Q. What was the first brick building erected in Portland?

A. Wadsworth-Longfellow House, at 487 Congress Street.

Q. Who once lived at 173 State Street in Portland?

A. Poet and prose writer John Neal (1793–1876).

Q. His paintings on the sides of trailer trucks have given recognition to what Winn artist?

A. Dale R. Rideout.

Q. Who sculpted the figure *Dead Pearl Diver,* part of the Sweat Museum's permanent collection in Portland?

A. Paul Akers.

Q. What is the name of author Kate Douglas Wiggin's home in Gorham?

A. Quillcote.

Q. Which artist, writer, and sculptor in Strong calls himself "the King of Tory Hill"?

A. Michael Rothschild.

———⊗⊗⊗———

Q. In 1937 who wrote *On Gilbert Head*?

A. Elizabeth Etnier.

———⊗⊗⊗———

Q. The letters of Rachel Carson were edited by what Portland woman?

A. Martha Freeman, whose book *Always, Rachel* was published in 1994.

———⊗⊗⊗———

Q. What was the name of the 1978–79 exhibit of Maine-made pottery at the Maine State Museum in Augusta?

A. *A Tradition in Clay.*

———⊗⊗⊗———

Q. In 1835 where did Longfellow write his travel sketches *Outre Mer*?

A. Emmons House, 25 Federal Street in Brunswick.

———⊗⊗⊗———

Q. For eighteen years what artist lived and worked year-round on Maine's Mohegan Island?

A. Andrew Winter (1893–1958).

———⊗⊗⊗———

Q. Which Maine artist does most of his painting in the winter?

A. Laurence Sisson, who says winter light is best for his seascapes and landscapes.

Q. Born in Head Tide, what Maine poet was a three-time Pulitzer Prize winner?

A. Edward Arlington Robinson.

Q. Who wrote *The Fastest Hound Dog in the State of Maine*?

A. John Gould, of Lisbon Falls.

Q. Set on the Maine coast, the Elm Island series books for boys was written by what Harpswell writer?

A. Elijah Kellogg.

Q. Who was elected president of the Society of Art in 1892?

A. Portland artist Harrison B. Brown.

Q. Born in Bangor in 1839, what artist is best known for her tabletop still lifes?

A. Anna Eliza Hardy.

Q. Who wrote the novel *Two If by Sea*?

A. Edward M. Holmes, of Winterport.

Q. Who wrote, "I have never been a member of any literary establishment. I am flying in the dark as much as a young person starting out"?

A. Bath poet Richard Aldridge (1930–1994).

Q. Who helped launch the official Maine Chapter of Romance Writers of America in 1995?

A. Best-selling novelist Tess Gerritsen *(Harvest)* of Camden.

Q. What is the title of Edgar Allen Beem's book about Maine art and artists?

A. *Maine Art Now* (1990).

Q. What was the title of the 1963 Colby College landmark art exhibit?

A. Maine and Its Role in American Art, 1740–1963.

Q. When did realist painter Alex Katz first come to Maine?

A. 1949, as a student at the Skowhegan School of Painting and Sculpture.

Q. In 1980 who painted the three-panel mural in the post office in Bangor?

A. Yvonne Jacquette.

Q. Which Cundy's Harbor poet was at one time the editor of the *Outlook,* a literary journal?

A. Harold T. Pulsifer.

Q. What shipwreck inspired Longfellow's poem "The Wreck of the *Hesperus*"?

A. The wreck of the schooner *Helen Eliza,* driven ashore west of Bailey Island, in 1869.

Q. What literary couple lived at Chimney Farm in Nobleboro?

A. Henry Beston *(The Outermost House)* and his wife, Elizabeth Coatsworth *(Maine Ways).*

Q. Which Cushing artist is known for his portraits of stones from the rockbound coast?

A. Alan Magee.

Q. Born on Whitehead Island, near Saint George, in 1884, who wrote the books of poetry *Inner Harbor* and *Maine Coast*?

A. Wilbert Snow.

Q. Where did Ben Ames Williams write his novel *Strange Woman*?

A. At his home in North Searsmont.

Q. Which English literary luminary stayed at the Bangor House in 1882?

A. Oscar Wilde.

Q. Novelist Mary Ellen Chase was born in 1887 in what town?

A. Blue Hill.

Q. Which Maine photographer is known for her portraits of the Paris and New York intellectual communities in the 1920s?

A. Berenice Abbott, who lived and worked at her cabin on the shores of Lake Hebron.

Q. Who founded the College of Music of Cincinnati?

A. George Ward Nichols, of Mount Desert Island.

Q. Who wrote the words to "America (My Country 'Tis of Thee)"?

A. Rev. Samuel Francis Smith, of Waterville.

Q. Where in Maine will you find a Gilbert Stuart portrait of George Washington?

A. Robinson Treasure Room of the Colby College Library, Waterville.

Q. Who wrote the poem "Open Secrets of Bowdoinham"?

A. Stephen Petroff, poet laureate of Bowdoinham.

Q. Which short story about a Maine tragedy won many awards for its author?

A. "The Ledge," written in 1958 by Lawrence Sargent Hall, of Orr's Island.

Q. Which Maine author wrote many books on ethics and Quaker history?

A. Rufus Jones, of South China (1863–1948).

Q. What York artist is best known for her floral paintings?

A. Beverly Hallam.

Q. Which composer was known as "the Handel of Maine"?

A. Supply Beicher, of Farmington (1751–1836).

Q. Which brother of a famous Maine poet composed hymns?

A. Samuel Longfellow.

Q. Sophie May was the pen name of what nineteenth-century Norridgewock author?

A. Rebecca Clarke.

Q. Who is known as Maine's first folklorist?

A. John Josselyn, who began writing about Maine in 1638.

Q. What fictional Maine town was created by writer William Clark?

A. Cedar River.

Q. What was one of the reasons given by novelist Erskine Caldwell for moving to Maine?

A. "I wanted to get as far away as possible from the Deep South so I could gain perspective."

Q. What inspired John Greenleaf Whittier to write his poem "Maud Muller"?

A. Riding a country road near South Berwick, he saw a young woman haying.

Q. Where will you find the largest collection of literary works by Maine women?

A. Abplanalp Library, Westbrook College.

Q. What was the subject of Ruth Moore's first novel, *The Weir*?

A. The story of a sardine fisherman on Moore's native Gott's Island.

SPORTS & LEISURE

C H A P T E R F I V E

Q. Who was the first full-blooded Native American to play major-league baseball?

A. Louis Sockalexis, a Penobscot born on Indian Island in 1873.

Q. Who fought in Maine's longest prize fight?

A. James O'Neil and James Fitts boxed bare-knuckle at North Berwick.

Q. What pitcher was dubbed "the fireballer of the New York Mets" in 1964?

A. Carlton Willey, of Cherryfield.

Q. First licensed in 1897, who was Maine's first registered female guide?

A. Cornelia Crosby, of Rangeley Lakes.

Q. When was the last Maine hunting season for caribou?

A. 1899, by which time they had almost vanished from the state.

Q. Who played shortstop for the Boston Red Sox in the 1903 World Series?

A. Fred Parent, of Sanford.

Q. Playing with the Chicago Nationals, what Hartland native led the National League in hitting in 1880?

A. George Gore.

Q. Since 1934 what group has governed Maine high school sports?

A. State Principals Association.

Q. Where was distance runner Joan Benoit Samuelson born?

A. Cape Elizabeth (in 1957).

Q. For what major-league team did Native American Louis Sockalexis play?

A. Cleveland Spiders, in the 1890s.

Q. Maine's longest bare-knuckle prize fight lasted how long?

A. Sixty-six rounds; four hours and twenty minutes.

Q. Who fought in Maine's shortest prize fight?

A. Al Couture and Ralph Walton in Lewiston, September 26, 1946. It lasted 10.5 seconds, including the referee's ten-second count.

Q. What years did Joan Benoit win the women's division of the Boston Marathon?

A. 1979 and 1982.

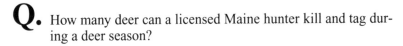

Q. What is Maine's most popular recreation area for swimming, hiking, and boating?

A. Acadia National Park on Mount Desert Island.

Q. How many deer can a licensed Maine hunter kill and tag during a deer season?

A. One.

Q. What is Maine's official state gamefish?

A. Landlocked salmon.

Q. How does a Maine moose hunter get a proper license?

A. By entering his or her name in the state moose lottery.

Q. What is deer jacking?

A. Illegally killing deer at night while blinding them with a bright light in their eyes.

Q. Who was Gadabout Gaddis?

A. A famous Maine fly-fisher.

Q. What is the Maine nickname for landlocked salmon?

A. "Mr. Silversides."

———⊶⊷———

Q. What percentage of Maine moose hunters kill a moose?

A. Better than 90 percent.

———⊶⊷———

Q. Where is Gadabout Gaddis Airport?

A. Gingham.

———⊶⊷———

Q. What is Maine's most popular white-water rafting river?

A. Kennebec.

———⊶⊷———

Q. When did Maine get its first indoor tennis courts?

A. 1968, on Route 1 in Falmouth.

———⊶⊷———

Q. What bowling alleys were billed as Maine's "first streamlined alleys"?

A. Biddeford's Twentieth Century Lanes, opened in 1938.

———⊶⊷———

Q. What is a Maine pung?

A. A boxlike sleigh drawn by a single horse.

Q. Who invented the famous Maine Hunting Boot?

A. Leon Leonwood Bean, when he returned from a hunting trip with sore, wet feet.

Q. Where can a person buy venison in Maine?

A. Nowhere. It is illegal to sell deer meat anywhere in the state.

Q. How much money did white-water rafters spend in Maine in 1996?

A. An estimated $12.3 million.

Q. How much money did L. L. Bean need to make his first one hundred pairs of Maine Hunting Boots?

A. Four hundred dollars.

Q. What does a Maine deer hunter mean when he says he shot a real "cruncher"?

A. He shot a very large deer.

Q. How many snowmobile clubs are in Maine?

A. 270, as of 1998, with more than 12,000 member families.

Q. Who was known as "the Babe Ruth of Maine"?

A. Del Bissonette, of Winthrop.

Q. At what age does an angler get a free Maine fishing license?

A. Seventy or older.

Q. What is the name of the athletic teams of Morse High School in Bath?

A. Shipbuilders.

Q. What anglers in Maine do not need a license?

A. Those who fish in tidal waters.

Q. What was Louis Sockalexis's best batting average with the Cleveland Spiders?

A. .331.

Q. Who are the Falcons?

A. Rumford High School athletic teams.

Q. When did the Waterville High School soccer team win its only state championship?

A. 1963.

Q. What was called "the greatest baseball game ever played in Maine"?

A. The October 21, 1910, game between the American League All Stars and the All-Maine Minor League Stars, played in South Portland.

Q. What is the name of the trophy awarded each year to the best high school football lineman?

A. Chet Bulger Award.

―――∞∞∞―――

Q. Where was board-game pioneer Milton Bradley born?

A. Vienna, Maine.

―――∞∞∞―――

Q. As of 1997, how many golf courses were in Maine?

A. 195.

―――∞∞∞―――

Q. How many white-water rafting locations are in Maine?

A. Fifteen, where rafting outfitters are available.

―――∞∞∞―――

Q. What river is best known for its wilderness canoe trips?

A. Allagash.

―――∞∞∞―――

Q. How long is the Allagash River from its source at Eagle Lake to its meeting with the Saint John River?

A. Sixty-two miles.

―――∞∞∞―――

Q. What will hikers in particular find appealing about Maine's Camden Hills State Park?

A. A four-and-half-mile hike that includes Mount Battie and Mount Megunticook, with splendid views of Penobscot Bay.

Q. What was the name of the 1930 Portland baseball team?

A. Hustlers.

Q. What do hikers find atop Acadia's Cadillac Mountain?

A. Gift shops and crowded parking lots.

Q. What Boston Red Sox catcher was known as "the Pride of Lewiston"?

A. Bill "Rough" Carrigan.

Q. Where in Acadia National Park are some of the best views of the ocean?

A. Atop the Pemetic Mountain ridge.

Q. What is Maine's third-highest mountain?

A. Old Speck, a hiker's favorite.

Q. The state had how many resident hunters as of 1991?

A. About 17,400.

Q. What is the nickname of the University of Maine's athletic teams?

A. Black Bears.

Q. How long had Maine's baseball program been in existence before it won the College World Series?

A. Seventy-nine years.

———❧———

Q. Mooselookmeguntick Lake has how many maintained camp sites?

A. Sixty, most accessible only by boat.

———❧———

Q. Where can hikers and mountain climbers find llamas to help carry gear?

A. Telemark Inn near Bethel.

———❧———

Q. How many wild turkeys are estimated to be in the state?

A. More than five hundred.

———❧———

Q. What is the average success rate for Maine's licensed deer hunters?

A. Just under 20 percent.

———❧———

Q. What special requirement, in addition to a license, must Maine deer and moose hunters comply with?

A. All hunters must wear blaze-orange clothing, including a hat.

———❧———

Q. What segment of Maine's Route 1 is closed to cyclists?

A. The section between Brunswick and Bath.

Q. In 1937 where was the America's Cup racing yacht *Ranger* built?

A. Bath Iron Works on the Kennebec River.

Q. Who coached the University of Maine baseball team in 1964, when it won its first Intercollegiate World Series?

A. Jack Butterfield.

Q. What pro football Hall of Famer was born in Rumford?

A. Chicago Cardinal tackle Chet Bulger.

Q. Where was major leaguer George F. "Piano Legs" Gore born?

A. Hartland, in 1855.

Q. Who managed the Bath Iron Works baseball team in 1942?

A. Former major-league catcher Val Picinich, of Nobleboro.

Q. What is the nickname of the Maine Maritime Academy's athletic teams?

A. Mariners.

Q. Who coached the University of Maine girls basketball team that won the America East Conference title in 1997?

A. Joanne Palombo-McCallie.

Q. The chief purpose of what organization is to enhance and conserve Maine's saltwater fisheries and resources?

A. Coastal Conservation Association of Maine.

Q. For what team did "Piano Legs" Gore play when he won a major-league batting title in 1880?

A. Chicago White Stockings.

Q. Who is Lawrence High School's most famous basketball player?

A. Cindy Blodgett, who led the girls team to four state titles.

Q. Where is Lawrence High School?

A. Fairfield.

Q. When can Maine's wild turkeys be hunted?

A. May, by limited permit only.

Q. When was the first documented baseball game played in Maine?

A. October 10, 1860.

Q. What is Maine's oldest sanctioned croquet tournament?

A. The annual Claremont Croquet Classic, sanctioned by the U.S. Croquet Association in 1978.

Q. What former Oakland Athletics shortstop was raised in Winterport?

A. Mike Bordick, who played with Oakland for four seasons until 1996, when he joined the Baltimore Orioles.

Q. What is Olympic medalist skier Picabo Street's home training ski area?

A. Sugarloaf USA.

Q. What major-league baseball team was managed by Carl "Stump" Merrill of Brunswick?

A. New York Yankees, in 1984.

Q. How tall was Carl "Stump" Merrill, former catcher at the University of Maine?

A. Five feet, eight inches.

Q. How many ski trails are at Maine's Sugarloaf USA ski area?

A. Seventy-one.

Q. What is the nickname of South Portland High School's athletic teams?

A. Riots.

Q. By what margin did Maine distance runner Joan Benoit lose the 2,000-meter Olympic Invitational race in 1983?

A. .01 second, to Patti Sue Plummer.

Q. How many girls basketball state championship teams did Cindy Blodgett play on?

A. Four, the total number of years she played for Lawrence High School.

Q. Who wrote *A Complete Guide to Catching Bass in Maine*?

A. Dave Barnes and Harry Vanderweide.

Q. What was the most popular Atlantic salmon fly in Maine in 1900?

A. The Jock Scott.

Q. What former star pitcher for the University of Maine pitched for the USA Summer Olympic baseball team in 1984?

A. Billy Swift.

Q. What is the nickname of the Brunswick High School athletic teams?

A. Dragons.

Q. What former pitcher for the Portland Sea Dogs was named the Most Valuable Player in the 1997 World Series?

A. Livan Hernandez, of the Florida Marlins.

Q. How long is Maine's hunting season for bobcats?

A. Two months; December 1–January 31.

Q. What is Maine's oldest saltwater fishing tournament?

A. Bailey Island Tuna Tournament, held each July.

Q. How many miles of cross-country ski trails are open at the Harris Farm Stand in Kennebunk?

A. About twenty.

Q. Who coached the Portland Pirates hockey team in the 1997–98 season?

A. Hockey Hall of Fame forward Bryan Trottier.

Q. What city was the site of the Cassius Clay–Sonny Liston heavyweight fight?

A. Lewiston.

Q. Who wrote *Was Baseball Really Invented in Maine?*

A. Will Anderson.

Q. Who is Bangor's best-known resident Boston Red Sox fan?

A. Novelist Stephen King.

Q. What is the nickname of Bowdoin College's athletic teams?

A. Polar Bears.

Q. Who was the World Junior Champion of Horseshoe Pitching in 1975?

A. Doug Kienia, of Kittery.

———∞———

Q. What ten-year-old won the world championship for two-baton twirling?

A. Rosemarie Samson, of Auburn, in 1975.

———∞———

Q. How many times did the Maine-built yacht *Ranger* win the America's Cup?

A. Four.

———∞———

Q. What snowmobile driver jumped nine cars?

A. Perry Kerry, of Portland, at Scarborough Downs on February 11, 1977.

———∞———

Q. How long did Bates College students play volleyball to make *The Guinness Book of World Records*?

A. Seventy-one continuous hours.

———∞———

Q. How far did Stan Lemelin and Rick Foss of Lewiston ride their motorcycles in twenty-four hours?

A. 1,142 miles, on July 27, 1977.

———∞———

Q. What was the nickname of the 1914 Lewiston New England League baseball team?

A. Cupids.

Q. Who won the women's javelin throw at the 1979 Junior AAU Olympics?

A. Kathy Calo, of York.

Q. Who founded the Claremont Croquet Classic?

A. Allen Lord McCue.

Q. Who was the women's national champion shot-putter in 1975?

A. Ann Turbyne, of Winslow.

Q. Where was Brooklyn Dodgers ace pitcher Sandy Koufax born?

A. Ellsworth.

Q. What is the nickname of the Portland professional hockey team?

A. Pirates.

Q. Who was the first woman in New England to compete in men's varsity intercollegiate athletics?

A. Ellen Shulman, a member of the Bowdoin College swimming team in 1972.

Q. Who was the strongest man in the world in the 1930s?

A. John B. Gagnon of Augusta, who held the world weight-lifting title.

Q. Who held the amateur world featherweight boxing title in 1885?

A. Jack McAulliffe, of Bangor.

———∞∞∞———

Q. Where was singer Robert Goulet when he forgot the words to the national anthem?

A. Lewiston, singing at the Clay-Liston heavyweight bout.

———∞∞∞———

Q. Who was the first person to cross the continent in a wheelchair?

A. George Murray, of Millinocket, in 1981.

———∞∞∞———

Q. How long did the Clay-Liston heavyweight championship bout in Lewiston last?

A. One minute, twelve seconds. Clay won by knockout.

———∞∞∞———

Q. How long is the Maine International Bicycle Race?

A. 105 miles, from Jackman to Waterville.

———∞∞∞———

Q. Where was the first eighteen-hole golf course in the nation?

A. Poland Spring, laid out in 1894.

———∞∞∞———

Q. How old was Lewiston's Joseph "Joey" Gamache when he became the U.S. Junior Olympic lightweight boxing champion in 1982?

A. Sixteen.

Q. What was the only unbeaten team in the 1981 Taiwan Youth Invitational Basketball Tournament?

A. The Maine Junior Boys.

Q. What was the nickname of Portland's first professional hockey team?

A. Maine Mariners.

Q. What was the first college baseball team from the East to win the Riverside National Intercollegiate Tournament in California?

A. University of Maine, in 1978.

Q. Where is the nation's oldest yacht club?

A. Lake Cobbosseecontee.

Q. What is the title of Joan Benoit's book?

A. *Running Tide.*

Q. Some of the richest purses in the nation are offered at what stock car race track?

A. Oxford Plains, in Oxford.

Q. What is the name of the harness racing grandstand at the Fryeburg fairgrounds?

A. John F. Weston Memorial Grandstand.

Q. Who played catcher when the University of Maine baseball team won the World Series of College Baseball in 1964?

A. Carl "Stump" Merrill, who made no errors and allowed no stolen bases.

———

Q. Which NASCAR race driver hails from Newburgh?

A. Ricky Craven.

———

Q. What is the nickname of the Wells High School athletic teams?

A. Warriors.

———

Q. When was the first horse race staged at the annual Cumberland Fair?

A. 1871.

———

Q. Competing in Maine's first documented baseball game were what teams (October 10, 1860)?

A. Sunrise Club of Brunswick and Bowdoin College Seniors.

———

Q. Where did President William Howard Taft play golf while he was visiting Maine?

A. Kebo Golf Club in Bar Harbor.

———

Q. What is the oldest continuously operating fair in North America?

A. Skowhegan Fair, which began in 1818.

Q. How many sanctioned harness racing tracks are in Maine?

A. Fourteen.

Q. Who won the Girls' National Free-Style Ski Championship in 1975?

A. Karen Colburn, of Bangor.

Q. When did the minor-league Maine Guides play their first baseball game in Maine?

A. April 18, 1984.

Q. What airport is closest to the state's best freshwater fishing?

A. Gadabout Gaddis Airport.

Q. Where was the thirteenth Annual World Heavyweight Ski Championship held?

A. Sugarloaf, in March 1981.

Q. What Maine skier was inducted into the National Ski Hall of Fame?

A. Wendell "Chummy" Broomhall, of Rumford, in 1981.

Q. The first balloon to cross the Atlantic took off from what place?

A. Presque Isle, in 1978.

Q. Where did President Dwight Eisenhower hook his first Maine brook trout?

A. Parmachenee Lake.

Q. The Claremont Classic Croquet court contains how many wickets?

A. Nine.

Q. Who set the distance record for dogsledding by covering twenty-three hundred miles from Fairbanks, Alaska, to Lewiston between November 1950 and April 1951?

A. Cecil "Mush" Moore, of Danville.

Q. How far did Dick Wallingford's two gray horses from West Forks pull twenty-two thousand pounds over dry clay?

A. Sixty-six and a half inches in 1981, a world record.

Q. Where do the Portland Sea Dogs play their home games?

A. Hadlock Field.

Q. How long is the longest pair of skis in the New Sweden Historical Society Museum?

A. Nine-plus feet.

Q. What are the most challenging rapids for Maine white-water kayakers?

A. Class V.

Q. Who is recorded as the first person to climb to the peak of New Hampshire's Mount Washington?

A. Jedediah Preble, a Portland businessman.

Q. Where were the Camp Fire Girls founded?

A. The Lake Sebago camps of Luther Halsey Gulick and his wife Charlotte Vetter Gulick, on March 17, 1912.

Q. What is the *Happy Hooker*?

A. A charter boat that fishes out of South Harpswell.

Q. When is ice fishing legal in Maine?

A. From the time the ice forms until March 31.

Q. What is the greatest outdoor danger facing people in Maine?

A. Hypothermia.

Q. In Maine what model bow is illegal to use for hunting?

A. Crossbow.

Q. A mascot named Slugger belongs to what team?

A. Portland Sea Dogs.

Q. What is the nickname of the Marshwood High School athletic teams?

A. Hawks.

Q. Where do the Portland Pirates play their home hockey games?

A. The Portland Civic Center.

Q. Who was the owner of the Maine-built racing yacht *Ranger*?

A. Harold "Mike" Vanderbilt.

Q. Huskies is the nickname for what institution's athletic teams?

A. Maine Central Institute.

Q. What baseball team competed in four consecutive College World Series?

A. University of Maine.

Q. How long are the annual dog-sled races at Greater Fort Kent?

A. The main event is 250 miles long.

Q. Maine, New Hampshire, Quebec, and New Brunswick contain how many miles of connecting snowmobile trails?

A. About 10,500.

Q. Who won the Calder Cup ice hockey trophy in 1978?

A. Maine Mariners.

Q. Who needs a Maine hunting license?

A. Every hunter sixteen years old and older.

Q. Who was the University of Maine's first baseball All-American?

A. Rick Bernardo, in 1986.

Q. How heavy are the draft-horse teams that compete at Maine's Cumberland Fair?

A. Not under twenty-eight hundred pounds and not over thirty-two hundred pounds.

Q. Where is the state's only curling club?

A. Belfast.

Q. How much does a curling stone weigh?

A. Forty pounds.

Q. What is the nickname of the Colby College athletic teams?

A. Mules.

Q. Who won ten Maine amateur golf championships, more than anyone else?

A. Mark Plummer, of Portland.

Q. When the University of Maine baseball team competed in the College World Series four consecutive years, who was the team's coach?

A. John Winkin.

Q. Who managed the Portland Sea Dogs in 1997?

A. Fredi Gonzalez.

Q. Where did the Maine Guides play their home games?

A. The Ballpark at Old Orchard Beach.

Q. What is the maximum-size shotgun that's legal for hunting in Maine?

A. Ten-gauge.

Q. How long did the minor-league Maine Guides play baseball in Maine?

A. From 1984 to 1988.

Q. Who can set traps without a license in Maine?

A. Persons under ten years old.

Q. Where was major-league shortstop George Henry "Topsy" Magoon born?

A. Saint Albans.

Q. What was the first major-league team to hire Topsy Magoon?

A. Brooklyn Bridegrooms, in 1898.

Q. Who wrote the book *Playing Like a Girl,* which is about Cindy Blodgett, Maine's best-ever girls basketball player?

A. Tabitha King.

Q. Where was major-league pitcher Robert William "Stanley Steamer" Stanley born?

A. Portland.

Q. What was the score of Maine's first documented baseball game (1860)?

A. Sunrise Club 46, Bowdoin College Seniors 42.

Q. Where is it illegal at all times to shoot deer in Maine?

A. Mount Desert Island.

Q. What are the best times of day to see Maine moose?

A. Dawn and dusk.

Q. Which University of Maine pitcher later played for the Houston Astros?

A. Bert Roberge.

———— ⌘ ————

Q. Where is organized broom hockey played?

A. At the annual White World Winter Carnival in Kingfield.

———— ⌘ ————

Q. Where is the highest cross-country ski center in New England?

A. Maine's Saddleback Mountain.

———— ⌘ ————

Q. What is Sail Maine?

A. A nonprofit organization that promotes sailing in Maine.

———— ⌘ ————

Q. What baseball teams played in the Centennial Fourth of July celebration games in Bangor in 1876?

A. Mutuals of Saint John and Bangor Orients.

———— ⌘ ————

Q. Who regulates sportsfishing for striped bass in Maine?

A. Department of Marine Resources.

———— ⌘ ————

Q. What sport did marathoner Joan Benoit first play at Cape Elizabeth High School?

A. Field hockey.

Q. How far off the Maine coast are most blue sharks hooked?

A. Beyond twenty miles.

———∞———

Q. What is the nickname of the Belfast High School athletic teams?

A. Lions.

———∞———

Q. Who coached the Bowdoin ice hockey team to their first Eastern Collegiate Athletic Conference Division II championship in 1971, when they defeated Vermont, 5-4?

A. Sid Watson.

———∞———

Q. What pitcher from Mexico, Maine, later played with the Mexico City Tigers in the Mexican League?

A. Stan Thomas.

SCIENCE & NATURE

C H A P T E R   S I X

Q. How many years has it been since a rattlesnake was seen in Maine?

A. One hundred, as of 1997.

Q. What Maine bird is also known as a sea parrot?

A. Atlantic puffin.

Q. What is the lobster's larger claw called?

A. Crusher.

Q. How many species of whales and porpoises have been sighted in the Gulf of Maine?

A. More than twenty.

Q. How many coyotes are in Maine?

A. Between ten and sixteen thousand.

Q. Why do northern shrimp *(Pandalus borealis)* visit the Maine coast?

A. To lay their eggs.

Q. What is the weight of a newborn black bear cub?

A. Between five and twelve ounces.

Q. How much does a black bear cub weigh at the end of its first summer?

A. From forty-five to ninety-five pounds.

Q. How many species of birds were recorded in Maine in 1995?

A. 419.

Q. What is the estimated size of Maine's herd of white-tailed deer?

A. Between two and three hundred thousand.

Q. Where is the best place on the Maine coast to watch for harlequin ducks?

A. Marginal Way in Ogunquit, during the winter.

Q. What is Maine's most commercially valuable inhabitant of the tidal flats?

A. The bloodworm, worth twenty dollars a pound and up.

Q. Where does Maine rank among states in bear population?

A. Second.

Q. When was the last passenger pigeon seen in Maine?

A. 1896, at Dexter.

Q. What is the Furbish lousewort?

A. A rare, fernlike snapdragon discovered by Maine botanist Kate Furbish.

Q. What is Maine's largest bird of prey?

A. Bald eagle.

Q. What is Maine's largest salamander?

A. Mudpuppy.

Q. During what months of the year do Maine winds blow their hardest?

A. March and November.

Q. What is the great-spangled fritillary, which turned up in Maine in great numbers during the early 1900s?

A. A butterfly (it has not returned since).

Q. How many black bears are in Maine?

A. An estimated ten thousand and increasing, as of 1998.

Q. What is Maine's smallest turtle?

A. Common musk turtle.

Q. What is the only hummingbird to visit Maine?

A. Ruby-throated.

Q. What tree was the key to Maine's early leather-tanning industry?

A. Hemlock.

Q. What is the only community in Maine that sets its own lobster-trapping season?

A. Monhegan Island.

Q. Who caught the only albino lobster taken in Maine waters?

A. Bill Coppersmith, of Raymond, on November 10, 1997.

Q. What insect has done the most damage to Maine's timber resource?

A. Spruce budworm.

Q. How many different types of flounder swim in Maine coastal waters?

A. Thirteen.

Q. Where are most of Maine's blueberries harvested?

A. Washington County.

Q. Where is Maine's largest gathering ground for wild waterfowl?

A. Merrymeeting Bay.

Q. What is the first bird known to have flown around the world?

A. A common tern, banded and released on July 3, 1913, at Maine's Eastern Egg Rock.

Q. Where was the nation's largest eastern white pine discovered?

A. Blanchard, in 1971. It was 147 feet high and more than 18 feet around.

Q. For whom was the Lincoln sparrow named?

A. Arthur Lincoln, of Dennysville, who discovered it in 1833.

Q. Which Maine lake has the largest number of islands?

A. Moosehead, with almost five hundred.

Q. Where in Maine is the most popular bald eagle nesting habitat?

A. Swan Island, in the Kennebec River.

———∞———

Q. Who made the first solar observation in North America?

A. Harvard professor Samuel Williams on October 27, 1780, at Isleboro.

———∞———

Q. What is Maine's most abundant and annoying insect?

A. The black fly.

———∞———

Q. What is the primary collection of the Nylander Museum in Caribou?

A. Maine shells and fossils collected by amateur naturalist Olaf Nylander.

———∞———

Q. Where is Maine's largest stand of jack pine?

A. Great Wass Island's 1,579-acre preserve, which includes a rare 500-acre stand of jack pine.

———∞———

Q. Where is the Asticou Azalea Garden?

A. Northeast Harbor, just off Route 3.

———∞———

Q. What is Maine's most aquatic snake?

A. The northern water snake *(Nerodia sipedon)*.

Q. When are most of Maine's bear cubs born?

A. Mid-January.

———— ❦ ————

Q. How many nights a year do northern lights glow on the Maine horizon?

A. Approximately thirty. Listen for increased static on your AM radio.

———— ❦ ————

Q. How many hours of sunshine does Maine average a year?

A. About twenty-five hundred, which works out to more than one hundred days' worth. That's about the same as Florence, Italy.

———— ❦ ————

Q. What is the average temperature of the Atlantic Ocean off York Beach?

A. Just under sixty degrees Fahrenheit.

———— ❦ ————

Q. Where in Maine are you most likely to see a moose?

A. Between Stratton and Rangeley, although moose are seen everywhere in the state.

———— ❦ ————

Q. What is the most common frog found in Maine's peatlands?

A. Wood frog.

———— ❦ ————

Q. What furry quadruped was once abundant in Penobscot Bay?

A. Sea mink, hunted to extinction.

Q. When is the Maine hunting season for coyotes?

A. Every day but Sunday.

Q. What is the name of the albino lobster discovered in Casco Bay in November 1997?

A. Lincoln.

Q. What is the best-known and most famous of Maine's woody plants?

A. White pine.

Q. Which kind of seal are you most likely to see along the Maine coast?

A. Harbor seal (there are more than seventy-five hundred).

Q. What are Maine's predominant hardwoods?

A. Beech, birch, maple, and white ash.

Q. What species of fish are Maine fishways designed to assist?

A. Atlantic sea-run salmon, landlocked salmon, brook trout, brown trout, alewives, and shad.

Q. How much does a full-grown Maine harbor seal weigh?

A. From 200 to 250 pounds.

Q. How many species of birds have been seen in Portland's Back Cove?

A. About two hundred.

———⊗⊗⊗———

Q. How many federal and state fish hatcheries are in Maine?

A. Ten.

———⊗⊗⊗———

Q. What is Maine's most popular saltwater game fish?

A. Striped bass.

———⊗⊗⊗———

Q. What are the best times to canoe the Saco River?

A. Late June, July, and August.

———⊗⊗⊗———

Q. How much does an adult moose weigh?

A. Up to twelve hundred pounds.

———⊗⊗⊗———

Q. What bird is most likely to turn up at a Maine bird-feeding station?

A. Chickadee, Maine's state bird.

———⊗⊗⊗———

Q. Where are you likely to find the rare dwarf birch?

A. The summit of Mount Katahdin.

Q. Why does Maine have many beaver dams?

A. It is against the law to disturb any part of a beaver dam.

Q. How many gray squirrels are in Maine?

A. About twenty million, or an estimated minimum of two per wooded acre.

Q. Which way does a weatherstick bend if rain is on the way?

A. Down.

Q. Christmas wreaths are most often made from what material?

A. Balsam branch tips.

Q. How many moose are in Maine?

A. At least twenty-five thousand and increasing, as of 1998.

Q. How many nature preserves are in Maine?

A. Thirty-one.

Q. Virginia creeper does not grow in what Maine county?

A. Washington.

Q. Where have walrus bones been discovered in Maine?

A. Penobscot Bay, at Orrington.

———————

Q. What is Maine's largest natural history organization?

A. Maine Audubon Society, at Gisland Farm in Falmouth.

———————

Q. Who wrote *A Birder's Guide to Maine*?

A. Elizabeth and Jan Pierson and Peter D. Vickery.

———————

Q. What is the record snowfall for Portland in one winter?

A. 141.5 inches, in 1970–71.

———————

Q. A prospector can get a list of places to pan for Maine gold from what agency?

A. Maine Geological Survey.

———————

Q. What percentage of Maine people report they have seen a moose?

A. 87 percent.

———————

Q. How often have Maine residents celebrated a "green" (snow-less) Christmas?

A. 50 percent of the time since weather records have been kept.

Q. What is Maine's official state insect?

A. Honeybee.

Q. How close do humpback whales get to the Maine coast?

A. Within a half mile.

Q. How many species of poison ivy grow in Maine?

A. Five, each poisonous to the touch.

Q. Henry David Thoreau made how many trips to the Maine woods?

A. Three, between 1846 and 1857.

Q. What did Wilhelm Reich study at his institute in Rangeley?

A. Renewable orgone energy.

Q. Where is the Peary-MacMillan Arctic Museum?

A. Brunswick, on the Bowdoin College campus.

Q. Who discovered and first prepared insulin to treat diabetes?

A. Canadian scientists Charles Best, who was born in West Pembroke, and Sir Frederick Banting.

Q. Black bears prefer what summer foods?

A. Blueberries, raspberries, blackberries, and wild cherries.

———❦———

Q. Where is the Audubon Ecology Camp?

A. Hog Island, in Maine's upper Muscongus Bay.

———❦———

Q. What birds are known as Maine's "winter finches"?

A. Pine grosbeaks, red- and white-winged crossbills, common redpolls, pine siskins, evening grosbeaks, and, rarely, hoary redpolls.

———❦———

Q. Where is the Eagle Field Research Station?

A. Steuben, where it conducts natural history seminars.

———❦———

Q. What are the names of the two timber wolves who visited the Maine State House in Augusta?

A. Indy and Koani.

———❦———

Q. Which is the largest of Maine's wading birds?

A. Great blue heron.

———❦———

Q. What is a Maine fisher's favorite meal?

A. Porcupine.

Q. How much weight do raccoons add just before winter?

A. Many double their body weight.

Q. What Maine nesting habitat is favored by more kinds of waterbirds then any other?

A. Offshore islands.

Q. The state contained how many bald eagles at the turn of the century?

A. An estimated two hundred.

Q. When do Maine eiders lay their eggs?

A. The last week in April.

Q. How thick is a black bear's hide when it's ready to hibernate through winter?

A. At least three inches thick with a four-inch layer of fat under it.

Q. How did the early Maine coastal fishermen attract herring to their nets?

A. The fished at night and lit pitch-pine torches to lure herring inshore.

Q. How far can a white-tailed deer swim?

A. Several have been found on Maine islands six or seven miles offshore.

Q. When do harbor seals in Maine give birth?

A. June.

Q. What is the most common carnivore found on Maine's many islands?

A. Mink.

Q. When were the Fox Islands named?

A. 1603, by English explorer Martin Pring, who sighted several foxes along their shores.

Q. How many different plants found on Mount Desert have been catalogued?

A. More than fifteen hundred.

Q. Where is the primary razorbill nesting site on the Maine coast?

A. Matinicus Island.

Q. How large was the great white shark taken off Eastport in November 1932?

A. Twenty-six feet long. It was thought to be the same shark that had previously attacked a fishing boat.

Q. When do bobolinks arrive in Maine?

A. Early May.

Q. Where is the best moose-watching spot in Oxford County?

A. Grafton Flats, a large mudhole beside Route 26.

Q. How many deer-management districts are in Maine?

A. Seventeen.

Q. How large is the Scarborough Marsh Wildlife Management Area?

A. More than sixteen hundred acres of fresh- and salt-water wetlands.

Q. What important North American game bird is protected in Maine?

A. Mourning dove.

Q. What large beetles eat Maine's spring peepers?

A. Diving beetles *(Dytiscidae)*.

Q. During what span of years was the double-crested cormorant wiped out as a Maine breeding species?

A. From 1880 to 1925.

Q. How long has the great blue heron been visiting the Maine coast?

A. More than forty million years, according to fossils found.

Q. What percentage of Maine's legal lobster population is trapped each year?

A. More than 90 percent.

———

Q. How many eider chicks were born on the Maine coast in 1997?

A. About two hundred thousand.

———

Q. Maine's first English settlers called whales by what name?

A. Sea hogs.

———

Q. When are you most likely to hear the courting calls of great horned owls?

A. At dusk, in January.

———

Q. What two whale species were hunted in the area by Native Americans?

A. Right whale and humpback.

———

Q. What organization works to ensure the natural return of the wolf to Maine?

A. Maine Wolf Coalition.

———

Q. What Maine frog can be frozen for up to six weeks and then fully recover as temperatures rise?

A. Wood frog.

Q. What three species of owls are commonly found in Maine?

A. Great horned, barred, and saw whet.

Q. What is the greatest source of nutrients that enrich the Gulf of Maine?

A. Maine rivers emptying into the gulf.

Q. When did the turkey vulture first nest in Maine?

A. The 1950s.

Q. When are Maine's raccoon cubs born?

A. April and May, depending on the arrival of warm weather.

Q. When does the rhodora bloom in Mount Desert's Great Meadow?

A. June.

Q. What is anchor ice?

A. Ice that accumulates on the underwater surfaces of Maine streams.

Q. Why are Gulf of Maine waters more green than blue?

A. They are rich in floating phytoplankton.

Q. When does the kestrel leave Maine for warmer climes?

A. September.

Q. Where in Maine can you find the gray tree frog?

A. Southern and central parts of the state.

Q. What is the Gulf of Maine's most abundant zooplankton?

A. Copepods.

Q. What is known as Mount Desert's loveliest flower?

A. The purple fringed orchis.

Q. What birds nest in underground burrows on Maine's islands?

A. Leach's petrels.

Q. What is Maine's only entirely terrestrial salamander?

A. Redback.

Q. What causes bowling-ball-size burls on Maine's seaside spruce trees?

A. Particles of sea salt forced under the bark by gale winds.

Q. When are Maine's eiders unable to fly?

A. August, when they shed their feathers.

———— ❧ ————

Q. How many of Maine's islands are used as nesting sites?

A. More than five hundred, by several million pairs of birds.

———— ❧ ————

Q. When was Maine's last wolf hunt?

A. 1815, on the shores of West Penobscot Bay.

———— ❧ ————

Q. What Maine museum has a lobster exhibit?

A. Maine Maritime Museum in Bath.

———— ❧ ————

Q. How many miles of nature trails are at the Laudholm Farm in Wells?

A. Seven, along with more than 250 species of birds.

———— ❧ ————

Q. What three species of marine turtles are found in the Gulf of Maine?

A. Loggerhead, Kemp's ridley, and leatherback.

———— ❧ ————

Q. How large is Maine's Great Heath?

A. About four thousand acres.

Q. Where is one of the best places to explore a Maine coastal salt pond?

A. Rachel Carson Salt Pond Preserve on Route 32, just north of New Harbor.

Q. When is the best bird watching in Aroostook County?

A. Between late April and early October.

Q. What is Maine's most biologically diverse river?

A. Allagash.

Q. What winged winter visitor are you likely to see at Maine's Bangor Airport?

A. Snowy owl.

Q. How old are the Kennebunk Plains?

A. Approximately twelve thousand years.

Q. What are the boundaries of the Gulf of Maine?

A. Nantucket Shoals and Cape Cod on the west and Cape Sable on the east.

Q. What endangered species spawns in the lower Kennebec River?

A. Shortnose sturgeon.

Q. What crop did Maine Native Americans once harvest in Merrymeeting Bay?

A. Wild rice.

Q. The common eider's favorite nesting site is on what island?

A. Libby.

Q. What is the only Maine conifer to shed its needles every autumn?

A. Tamarack, or hackmatack.

Q. Where on the coast are you most likely to see a right whale?

A. Off Eastport.

Q. Which Maine bird of prey has a preference for snakes?

A. Broad-winged hawk.

Q. Portland's shortest day has how many hours of daylight?

A. A little fewer than nine.

Q. When are the first Maine tomatoes of the season most likely to ripen?

A. Last week of July or first week of August.

Q. When does the osprey first return to its Maine nesting sites?

A. Last week in March.

———— ∞∞∞ ————

Q. What is the world's largest living turtle?

A. Leatherback.

———— ∞∞∞ ————

Q. What is Maine's most accessible Atlantic puffin nesting site?

A. Eastern Egg Rock, at the mouth of Muscongus Bay.

———— ∞∞∞ ————

Q. What type of colorfully named fish, many weighing more than one thousand pounds each, congregate off Casco Bay in July?

A. Bluefin tuna.

———— ∞∞∞ ————

Q. What is the Maine woodcock's favorite food?

A. Earthworms, which make up more than four-fifths of their diet.

———— ∞∞∞ ————

Q. What is Maine's most popular game bird?

A. Ruffed grouse.

———— ∞∞∞ ————

Q. What is Maine's largest snake?

A. Black racer, which can be more than six feet long.

Q. What is a quahog?

A. Hard-shelled clam.

Q. The first leaves to turn red in the fall are on what Maine tree?

A. Smooth sumac.

Q. Which turtle was declared an endangered species in Maine in 1986?

A. Box turtle.

Q. Which Maine waterfowl are the first to head south in the fall?

A. Blue-winged teal, which depart in late August and early September.

Q. When is the best time to watch for the male woodcock's courting flights?

A. Dusk and dawn, near an open field, in late April and early May.

Q. What is the most abundant reptile in Maine?

A. Garter snake.

Q. Which turtle is said to be Maine's most attractive?

A. Painted turtle *(Chrysemys picta)*.

Q. How many hours of daylight are in Portland's longest day?

A. Almost sixteen.

Q. What is Maine's northernmost nesting site for piping plovers and least terns?

A. Reid State Park, at the southeast end of Georgetown Island.

Q. What is Maine's most frequently seen cetacean?

A. Harbor porpoise.

Q. What Maine harbor seal is the hero of a book about it?

A. Andre, of *Andre the Seal.*

Q. When do monarch butterflies migrate south along the Maine coast?

A. Late September and October.

Q. How many wild Canada geese spend their winters in Maine?

A. About two thousand, as of 1997–98.

Q. How many gray seals, also known as horsehead seals, visit eastern Maine?

A. About one hundred each summer.

Q. What commercial activity has reduced the Maine fisher population?

A. Clearcutting.

Q. When do orioles begin building their hanging nests in Maine?

A. Second week in May.

Q. What is Maine's most abundant diving bird?

A. Black guillemot.

Q. Why did early Maine settlers ferry their sheep to islands?

A. To protect them from wolves.

Q. Which Maine hawk flies closest to the ground while hunting?

A. Northern harrier.

Q. What is Maine's largest state park?

A. Baxter, at two hundred thousand acres.

Q. What are elvers?

A. Infant American eels that migrate up Maine's freshwater rivers in early spring.

Q. What river provides the best Atlantic-salmon fishing in the nation?

A. Penobscot River.

Q. How many wildlife management areas are in Maine?

A. Twenty-one.

Q. How long has it been since a black bear has been seen on a Maine island?

A. About 150 years.

Q. How many pounds of shad were once taken annually from Maine rivers?

A. Approximately three million pounds, in the early nineteenth century.

Q. Where is the Quaquajo Nature Trail?

A. Aroostook State Park.

Q. What is your best strategy if you meet a bear in the Maine woods?

A. Back away slowly. Do not run.

Q. What Maine predators have a taste for house cats?

A. Coyotes, the fishers, and great-horned owls.

Q. When were red foxes set free on No Man's Land, a thirty-acre Maine island?

A. 1916.

———— ❦ ————

Q. What is the life span of Maine's cold-water shrimp?

A. About five years.

———— ❦ ————

Q. What farm animal is most often attacked by Maine's black bears?

A. Sheep.

———— ❦ ————

Q. How do harbor seals communicate with their pups?

A. They bark.

———— ❦ ————

Q. For how long have ospreys used the nest at Pulpit Harbor?

A. A little more than a century.

———— ❦ ————

Q. How are Maine's bald eagles surveyed?

A. From light aircraft, as eagles have no fear of airplanes.

———— ❦ ————

Q. Where is Moosehorn National Wildlife Refuge?

A. Washington County.

Q. Where do Maine woodcock sleep on summer nights?

A. Open fields and meadows.

Q. Where is some of the best bird watching in mid-coast Maine?

A. Popham Beach State Park.

Q. What is the Maine shrimp's long, sharp beak called?

A. Rostrum.

Q. How do Maine chickadees remember where they store all the seeds they collect?

A. They grow extra memory neurons as winter approaches.

Q. Where can you find one of Maine's largest and most varied types of beaches?

A. At Popham Beach.